50

Trail Runs in

WASHINGTON

50

Trail Runs in

WASHINGTON

Cheri Pompeo Gillis

THE MOUNTAINEERS BOOKS

Published by
The Mountaineers Books
1001 SW Klickitat Way, Suite 201
Seattle, WA 98134

© 2002 by Cheri Pompeo Gillis

First edition, 2002

Published simultaneously in Great Britain by Cordee, 3a DeMontfort Street, Leicester, England, LE1 7HD

Manufactured in the United States of America

Project Editor: Laura Slavik
Editor: Brenda Pittsley
Cover and Book Designer: Kristy L. Welch
Layout Artist: Jennifer LaRock Shontz
Mapmaker: Jerry Painter
Photographers: Ron Nicholl, Cheri Pompeo Gillis, Doug Beyerlein, Pete Gillis

Cover photograph: © IndexStock Imagery, Bob Winsett, *Running up mountain trail*
Frontispiece: *A viewpoint of Ollalie Lake (Run 20) and Doug Beyerlein*

Library of Congress Cataloging-in-Publication Data

Gillis, Cheri Pompeo, 1952–
    50 trail runs in Washington / by Cheri Pompeo Gillis. — 1st ed.
        p.   cm.
Includes index.
    ISBN 0-89886-715-0 (pbk.)
    1. Running—Washington (State)—Guidebooks. 2. Trails—Washington (State)—Guidebooks. 3. Washington (State)—Guidebooks. I. Title:
Fifty trail runs in Washington. II. Title.
GV1061.22.W2 G55 2002
796.42'09797—dc21
                                                        2001006845

 Printed on recycled paper

CONTENTS

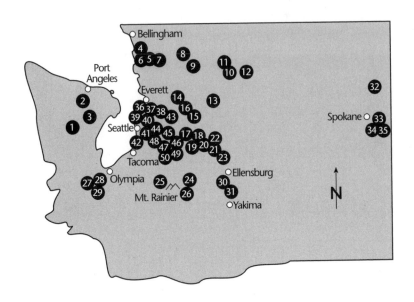

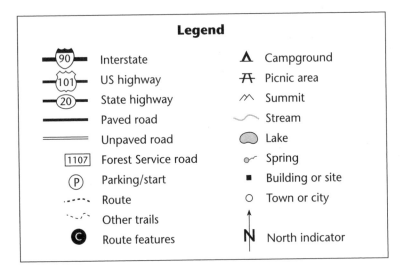

Legend

—(90)— Interstate	▲ Campground
—(101)— US highway	⊼ Picnic area
—(20)— State highway	⌒⌒ Summit
—— Paved road	⌒ Stream
═══ Unpaved road	⬭ Lake
[1107] Forest Service road	⌒ Spring
Ⓟ Parking/start	■ Building or site
⋯⋯ Route	○ Town or city
⌐⌐ Other trails	
⬤ Route features	N North indicator

ACKNOWLEDGMENTS

I would like to thank the following people for their help bringing this guide to successful completion. I never would have started such an ambitious project without the support and enthusiasm of Ron Nicholl. Doug Beyerlein spent many hours proofreading text and checking maps and photos for accuracy. Lynne Werner was always available for distant runs when I needed company. Many people shared their favorite routes with me and made time to accompany me on the trails, including Bill McKimmie, Steve Wells, Nancy Hautala, Bill Hughey, Steven Pierce, David Lygre, Dan Kuperberg, Ian Gillis, Frank Fleetham, Lynn Yarnall, Janine Duplessis, Karen King, Marlis DeJongh, Max Welker, Lary Webster, John Wagner, Tony Covarrubias, Scott Jurek, Jim Kerby, and Scott McCoubrey.

Thanks also to Jim Whiting, Martin Rudow, and Stephanie Irving for connecting me with The Mountaineers Books, Margaret Foster for accepting my proposal, and Cassandra Conyers, Brenda Pittsley, and Laura Slavik for carrying the project through to publication. And finally, I'd like to thank my husband, Peter, and children, Maureen, Marissa, and Ian, for their constant support and encouragement.

The Brink Trail on Tiger Mountain's Tradition Plateau (Run 46)

INTRODUCTION

The Cascade Mountains, the coastal ranges, the Columbia River, and the Pacific Ocean give Washington state some of the most beautiful and varied trails in the United States. The forests are crisscrossed with backcountry routes, making the region a veritable playground for trail runners. In addition to the abundant wilderness, the rails-to-trails movement, which converts abandoned rail beds into public trails, along with a number of large, forested city parks, translates into plenty of opportunities for getting away from it all even in urban areas.

This guide, written by a trail runner for trail runners, describes some of the best places in Washington to get out on the trail and have fun.

On the Pacific Northwest Trail (Run 6)

TRAIL RUNNING AND YOU

Putting your feet on the soft, forgiving dirt of the trail. Drinking in the scents of the evergreen forest. Hearing the chatter of birds and the babble of swiftly running brooks. These things offer respite from the work-a-day world. Whether your work is in a cubicle in a high-tech office building, involves working with the public, or focuses on the endless chores of household management and childcare, it's nice to get away to the trails.

The popularity of trail running has grown at an amazing rate in recent years. One indicator of this is the range of trail-specific footwear now available. Trail runners used to have two shoe choices: road running shoes with poor ankle support or clunky, low-cut hiking boots. But most running shoe manufacturers now offer shoes made specifically for trails. Trail races grace the covers of running magazines, trail running has its own magazine, and muddy runners are featured in ad campaigns for sportswear companies. What's the attraction?

WHY RUN ON TRAILS?

Running on trails awakens a sense of adventure. The trail environment changes constantly. The trail can be hard-packed and fast, muddy and slow, or snow-covered and icy. The forest landscape transforms drastically from season to season. The foliage is fresh and green in the spring with liberal sprinklings of wildflowers on the hillsides. In summer, it can feel like you're trudging though a jungle. By fall, the foliage starts to thin again, and come winter the stark landscape opens to fabulous views. In all seasons and at all times of the day, sun or rain filter through the vegetation from different angles creating different patterns. On runs in the city, tuning out the environment can be hard work. But in the woods, the pleasing environment makes it easy to tune out the rest of the world for a workout that is mentally and physically refreshing.

The physical benefits derived from running on trails are greater than those gained from running on pavement. Dirt is easier on the feet and joints than asphalt. The constant turning and twisting to avoid roots, rocks, low hanging branches, and streams firms the abdomen and upper body. Ankle tendons become stronger. And trail running in the Northwest provides a better workout for the feet, legs, and buttock muscles than even the ultimate StairMaster can muster.

You can be a trail runner at any age. As speed begins to decline with age, endurance increases. People find they can run and race longer distances. The opposite side of the "empty nest syndrome" is the joy of having more time for trails and "stomping around out in nature," as my teenage son calls it. And trail running offers you the ability to see more terrain than hiking does—an 8-mile hike is a full-day affair, but it's just a quick two-hour jaunt for the trail runner.

Although you can be a trail runner without running extensive distances, ultrarunning, which is anything beyond the 26.2 miles of a marathon, can bring athletes new challenges, new achievements, new friends, and a renewed sense of fun. After meeting the wonderful ultrarunners enjoying themselves on the trails, you may find that you want to join them. If so, you'll find encouragement in *UltraRunning* and *Trail Runner* magazines and on the Internet, where a search will turn up many long-distance trail races in the Northwest. Several Northwest ultra races are listed in the appendix of this book.

This guide is intended to tell you where to run trails, not how. Our ancestors had to run to get food and to avoid being food, so trail running is mostly a natural and intuitive activity. For the not-so-intuitive part of the process, however, some simple basics for running trails are outlined in the following section.

TRAIL RUNNING TIPS

Anyone can run on trails, whether you're a fair-weather jogger or a daily runner. You just have to be willing to mix walking with running, especially at first. Even the most talented trail runners sometimes walk.

New trail runners also should be aware that a 5-mile run on trails usually takes longer than a 5-mile run on the road. I frequently have encountered new runners who told friends and family they would be back from a 10-mile run in, say, two hours, yet they had gone only halfway in two hours. Gaining 1000 feet in a mile, which is quite common in the Cascade Mountains, can triple your normal pace time. Be sure to allow extra time for the climbs and the possibility of skirting fallen trees and other trail obstructions. Since it's very difficult to store enough energy for long trail runs, you need to schedule time to eat (see the Nutrition and Hydration section to follow). Experienced trail runners frequently eat while walking the steep sections, thereby leaving the runnable sections of the course for just that.

Trail running requires strength, balance, coordination, and focus. Constantly scan the trail to anticipate any fancy footwork necessary to avoid obstacles. Pay special attention to the area from 3 to 10 feet in front of you, with an occasional glance about 40 feet ahead. At first, run the parts that you feel comfortable running and walk the parts where you feel a need to be more careful. If you keep it up, your confidence will improve and soon you'll be leaping over obstacles without slowing down.

Falling is common in trail running. To keep their sense of humor about these tumbles, my Northwest trail running friends have set up a point system. Most falls are forward on the trail as a result of tripping over a root or rock. These falls, which generally just get you dirty, are worth 2 points. Some groups insist on the presence of blood to earn a full 10 points for a fall, but in my circle you can earn 10 points for a face plant in mud.

Most of the advanced trails listed in this guide can be hiked instead of run if you are a beginner; just be sure that you can cover the distance in the time you have available. A trail that is listed as a three-hour run can be a six-to-eight-hour hike. Take plenty of provisions and know what time sunset will be before you start on your trip.

Running downhill in the mountains can be very hard on the quadriceps because of the amount of force discharged with each landing. Putting on the brakes while running downhill is harder on the quadriceps than simply relaxing into a controlled fall. As you run, lean slightly forward. Let each foot make only brief contact with the trail so that your full weight doesn't crash down on your foot with each step. Jump over rocks and logs. If you misplace a foot, move quickly to the next foot. Some people run with an internal soundtrack of music from the 1960s through the 1990s. My song for downhill running is "Not to Touch the Earth" by The Doors.

Some competitive trail runners speedwalk up hills. Many of them can walk uphill faster than others can run. With posture erect, push yourself up the hill as fast as possible. Experiment with different stride lengths and arm positions. Walking up steep hills and running the flatter and downhill portions of a trail is a common practice.

CLOTHING AND SHOES

Clothing: Comfortable, nonbinding clothes and fabrics that wick away moisture are key to running year-round. In winter, layers of high-tech fabrics are great for keeping you warm and dry because they retain their insulating properties even when damp. Unfortunately, all the 100-percent-cotton tee shirts given out at races and other events only get wet and heavy in Northwest weather and can contribute to hypothermia. Do not wear them on trail runs. Change into them after the run.

I have yet to find a breathable jacket that will keep me dry through four hours of rain. Although a Polartec pullover is not waterproof, the rain seems to collect on the outside while you stay warm inside. A rain vest is also a nice option. In the Northwest, it is usually fairly warm when it's raining, so a vest will keep your trunk dry without making you too warm. A waterproof jacket is fine when it's colder and windy.

Socks: Durable socks with wicking properties are best for the trails. Many trail-running socks are available in colors other than white, for good reason. Trying to return socks to something like a shade of white after a few trips on Northwest trails takes more time and effort than the actual running. Gaiters keep rocks, sticks, dirt, sand, and other trail debris out of your shoes. I generally wear lightweight gaiters that fit over the shoe and stop just above the ankles. Longer versions are available for snow.

Hats and Gloves: Bring a lightweight running hat or cap on your run. In rain, the hat will keep the water out of your eyes. A hat also helps conserve body heat in the cold. And, on those rare occasions when the sun is out, a hat will protect your face from sunburn. Lightweight, polypropylene gloves are required equipment in the cold and wet. Take them with you even if you don't think you need them when you start out.

Trail Running Shoes: Good fit is the first requirement of a running shoe. It's okay to start out trail running in your street running shoes if they have good traction, but most shoe manufacturers now offer shoes made specifically for trail running. Trail running shoes have harder soles and toe guards for protection from rocks and roots, both underfoot and in places that you might kick. Because the foot can slide forward on steep downhill sections, extra toe room is advisable. If you need shoes that correct for pronation, supination, high arches, or any other issue, they are probably available in a trail shoe. Go to a reputable running store and have them help you with trail shoe choices. If you wear orthotics, take them with you and wear socks that are the same thickness as the socks you plan to use for trail running.

A good shoe store will let you run around the store or up and down the sidewalk in front of the store to check the fit in action. If your toes touch the end of the shoe when you run in it, it is too small. Lateral support can provide stability and help prevent rolling the ankle (your ankles will get stronger as your trail running progresses).

SAFETY AND NAVIGATION

A compass, map, altimeter, wristwatch, and GPS will help you successfully find your way on mountain trails. Know how to use these tools before starting out. Begin your run with the course traced on a map that includes elevation gradients. If you lose the trail because of

Wallace Falls (Run 15)

snow or fog, or come to an unmarked branch in the trail, use the watch to approximate your distance into the course and use the altimeter to help determine your current position on the map. Then use the compass to determine which direction the trail should be heading at that point. It is sometimes necessary to fan out across the area a little bit to find the trail. Orienteering classes are recommended for learning to navigate through unknown territory.

Flashlights: Keeping an emergency flashlight in your pack is easier than ever with the advent of LED lights. A single LED and battery unit about the size of a quarter can be purchased for a few dollars. This little item generates enough light to get you out of the forest when you hadn't planned on running in the dark.

For planned night running, several light options are available. I use small, handheld scuba diving lights. They're very bright and the beam allows you to see far ahead when you need to find trail markers. The one drawback of the diving lights is that the batteries last only three to four hours, so if you are doing a 100-mile trail run, you have to have a backup light and several sets of fresh batteries. The LED lights can get you through the night and more without changing batteries. They come in many configurations, including handheld lights and headlamps that are very light and easy to wear. The light emitted by an LED is more diffuse and the beam doesn't reach as far as diving lights, but I have used them for nighttime runs of up to twelve hours and find them suitable for everything but finding distant trail markings. For this, I still carry one small diving light.

Night running is a totally different experience from running during the day. It is cooler in the summer and, if you're away from urban areas, the stars can seem incredibly bright and close. On trails with roots and rocks, you need to slow down a little. The night air can become suddenly cold at higher altitudes, so bring extra clothing. Even the popular trails will be empty at night, so always run with a partner. Some people run at night just for the pleasure of it and some run at night for training. Most people who enter 100-mile races will be running through the night. If you have problems staying awake, you might try coffee, cola, or other caffeine drinks. These are usually available at aid stations in races. If that doesn't seem to help, arrange to have a pacer accompany you through the night. Sleepwalking off a cliff makes for a good story, but it seriously cuts into your race time.

Will Help Arrive? I don't recommend running alone on a remote trail. Run with a friend or a local running group. If nothing else, tell someone where you are going and when you expect to be back. For safety in numbers, some of the trails listed in this guide are frequented by hikers and other runners. Although it is a bit of an inconvenience to slow down or move over for other trail traffic, it is good to know that if you are injured on the trail someone will likely pass by and be able to alert authorities.

I have heard stories about runners who broke a leg or badly sprained an ankle and applied a splint using fallen tree limbs and a tee shirt, and walked out. The clothes that you need to keep yourself warm for the exertion level you expect to maintain will not be enough to keep you warm if you're injured and need to wait for help or walk out slowly, so keep that extra trash bag or jacket in your pack just in case. If you have trouble and can get yourself to a campground or see other hikers, tell them you need help. Don't try to walk through sprains and other injuries when there is help available. The help may no longer be there when you realize you really do need it. You can carry a cellular phone in areas where cellular service is available. The Issaquah Alps, Tiger, Squak, and Cougar Mountains are topped with telecommunications antennas; however, there are spots without coverage on these mountains, too. Try to know where you are at all times in case you need to tell a search-and-rescue person how to find you. On remote trails, always run with a friend. Most dogs are just not as good as Lassie when it comes to bringing back help.

The Ten Essentials: Your running pack should include extra clothing, extra food, sunglasses, a first-aid kit, a flashlight, a knife, a firestarter, matches in a waterproof container, a map, and a compass. Additionally, you should carry identification, money, aspirin, toilet paper (in a waterproof bag), and a large garbage bag with holes cut for arms and head.

The first-aid kit is for those 10-point falls. The identification and money are useful in emergencies (as is a medical insurance card). Aspirin can help with those small aches and pains or when you run into that overhanging tree limb. The large garbage bag can be converted into an emergency raincoat if the weather takes a turn for the worst. Remember when you are running that you are a long way from help. Be self-reliant and careful.

NUTRITION AND HYDRATION

Food: It's always a good idea to have energy bars or sports gels stashed in your pack for those times when a run lasts longer than expected. For planned long runs, you may wish to add food such as string cheese, sandwiches, or whatever it is that you like to eat while running.

A wooded path winds through Chuckanut Mountain (Run 4).

Some runners bring potato chips and beef jerky to help ensure they have adequate salt while running. Eating while running is something you need to train for. The longer the distance, the more important it is to eat during your run. If you are considering racing, try out different foods during training that might be available at race aid stations so you know whether they agree with you on a run. Typical aid station foods include peanut butter and jelly sandwiches, boiled potatoes, cheese, fruit, candy, pretzels, chips, cookies, turkey, hamburgers, and pizza. Learn what works for you.

Water Carriers: Water and electrolyte drinks can be carried in bottles that sit in holsters around the waist or in a bladder secured in a vest, belt, or backpack with a tube for drinking. Both the bottle packs and bladder packs have storage areas for extra clothes and safety equipment. Hydration vests have a larger water-carrying capacity and distribute the weight higher on the back, but they are somewhat harder to fill and clean. Double-bottle packs have pockets that are more accessible and give you the option of carrying an electrolyte drink in one bottle and plain water in the other. A handheld bottle works well for runs under two hours or if you know there are frequent water stops. Neoprene straps are available to secure a bottle to your palm. Bottles are easy to clean in the dishwasher. Use a hydration vest for long runs with no support or in areas lacking water sources. Use the double-bottle pack for runs where you can refill your bottles or on shorter runs. Many trail runners carry a hand-held bottle in addition to a bladder pack because they find that they drink more often and stay better hydrated if the bottle is in their hand.

Emergency Water: Natural water sources are plentiful in the west slopes of the Cascades, but it is a good idea to use a water purifying system or iodine to protect against viruses, bacteria, and Giardia infections. Although iodine tastes bad, it is convenient to carry. Iodine tablets kill everything but Cryptosporidium, which causes no symptoms in most of the people who ingest it. For others, Cryptosporidiosis can cause diarrhea, abdominal cramping, nausea, vomiting, fever, and headaches. If your immune system is not compromised, particularly from AIDS, Cryptosporidiosis will usually resolve itself within two weeks.

Use one iodine tablet per quart unless the water is dirty or very cold, then use two. It takes about fifteen to twenty minutes for the tablets to work, longer when the water is cold or dirty. To best protect yourself against Giardia, double the prescribed dose or double the recommended waiting time. Citrus drinks can be used to mask the taste, but should be added only after the iodine has had the required time to kill all the microbes. Ascorbic acid interferes with how iodine chemically purifies the water. Replace your supply of iodine tablets every year, as they lose their effectiveness.

Filtering is another water purifying option. Ceramic filters with microscopic passages remove everything but viruses, which are too small for the filter to capture. Viruses have to be killed with iodine tablets or boiling. Filters can clog easily and may be difficult to clean depending on the design. Try to use water where the silt or sand has already settled to the bottom.

Purifiers also use ceramic filters, but they have been impregnated with an iodine compound. The filter mechanically removes bacteria and parasites. Then the iodine kills any viruses. This is the most effective treatment available. The amount of iodine is less than what you would get from a tablet and therefore the water tastes better. In some purifiers you have to use a great amount of force to push the water through the filter prior to drinking it. This can be annoying when you're tired and very thirsty. Desirable design features in a filter or purifier include small size and weight, low force to use, ease of cleaning, field-replaceable cartridge, and a high flow rate of treated water.

UNFRIENDLY PLANTS AND ANIMALS

When I read about hiking and trail running in other parts of the country, I am struck by all the hazards: snakes, poison oak, ticks, etc. Many mountain trails in the Northwest are free of these concerns. There are no poisonous snakes in western Washington. Poison oak is comparatively rare, and the risk of Lyme disease from ticks is very small. Nonetheless, these and other hazards do exist.

Poison Oak: Learn to recognize poison oak. It generally grows in the underbrush, particularly in central and eastern Washington. The leaves are similar to oak leaves, but more rounded on the edges and shinier. The leaves grow in clusters of three, hence the phrase "Leaves of three, let it be." Preventive lotions that form a barrier on the skin are available in drugstores. Try one of these if you know you're going to be running in an area that has a lot of poison oak.

The first symptom of poison oak is a severe itching of the skin, usually appearing 24 to 48 hours after exposure. Later, a red inflammation and blistering occur. In severe cases, oozing sores develop. The rash spreads through contact with the poisonous sap, not as the result of contamination from sores. Although extremely irritating, most cases disappear in a week or 10 days. In the meantime, relief may be found through the application of medications available in most drugstores.

A physician should examine severe rashes, however, especially those covering large areas or accompanied by an above-normal body temperature. Medical treatment is most effective before the oozing sores appear.

Wash infected skin as soon as possible with cold water to minimize the severity of the rash and prevent the spread of the sap to uninfected parts of the body. Unfortunately, your skin absorbs the active compounds in the sap within the first three minutes, and you cannot prevent the dermatitis without medical treatment. Soap and water are superior to water alone in removing the sap, but they also temporarily remove a natural protective layer that helps keep the active compounds from being absorbed through the skin. Decontaminate clothing by laundering with soap or detergent. Wear protective gloves when handling contaminated shoes, gaiters, and clothing.

Cougars, Bears, and Rattlesnakes: Small black bears occasionally make an appearance looking for food, but they do not see you as food and will generally amble away unless taken by surprise or they see you as a threat to their cubs. I once encountered a black bear while camping. I banged a pot and spoon together until it turned around and walked slowly away. I have seen fresh black bear scat on trails, and named the bears Huckleberry and Blackberry (they do not chew their food very well). Yet in the many hours I've spent running on trails, I've never come close to a bear.

The general approach to dealing with black bears is to continue on calmly if the bear hasn't noticed you; back away slowly if it has seen you. Don't turn your back on the bear. Don't do anything that will make the bear feel cornered. Give it plenty of room to get away from you. Keep your voice low and calm. Sometimes a bear may stand up to better pick up your scent. Don't view this as aggression. If you are sure the black bear is attacking (very unlikely), throw your arms up in the air, act angry, scream at it, throw things at it; FIGHT BACK! If it's not attacking, but only moving toward you, loudly tell it to go away. Don't throw things at it. It's better not to make it angry.

Although cougar sightings are rare, their numbers are increasing in the state. Sightings and encounters have become more common, even near populated areas. In the wild, cougars prey on small or injured animals, so stand as tall as you can and stick with your group so you don't look like a straggler. When you're running, you look like prey. Make noise while running so you don't surprise animals coming around a curve. Do not approach cougar kittens, dead animals, or the cougar itself. If faced with a cougar, stand still, then slowly back away. If the cougar comes after you, fight back with rocks, sticks, or anything you have. Give the cougar an escape route. Do not crouch or turn your back on the cougar.

Rattlesnakes are common in Eastern and Central Washington. This is another animal that will avoid you if it can. If you plan to run in rattlesnake-infested areas, find out about anti-venom and emergency care from a local health care facility in advance.

Ticks: Ticks are more prevalent in Eastern Washington than in Western Washington. If you are running through brush and become aware of a slight irritation, look for a tick. It takes a few hours to burrow into the skin, so you can remove it more easily if you catch it early. The best way to remove a tick is with fine-pointed tweezers. Grasp the tick as closely to the skin as possible and pull straight back, using steady but gentle force. Do not use your fingers to remove the tick unless you're wearing protective gloves. Do not twist the tick, which can cause breakage, leaving part of its body in your skin. Do not crush, prick, or burn the tick, which may cause it to salivate or regurgitate infected fluids. Trying to smother the tick with products such as petroleum jelly or mineral oil doesn't work. Ticks can store enough oxygen to complete feeding. Consult your physician if you develop fever, headache, rash, or muscle aches, which are the symptoms of Lyme disease.

Yellow Jackets: Yellow jackets are flying insects that look like bees, but are much more likely to sting (or actually bite) a runner. They usually nest in the ground and are easily disturbed by a passing runner. Usually the first runner in a group gets the yellow jackets excited and the second and following runners get bitten. Unlike a honeybee that can only sting once, a single yellow jacket can bite a runner multiple times.

Some people have strong allergic reactions to yellow jacket bites, including swelling, constricted breathing, and even death. If you are allergic to yellow jackets, consult your physician before going out on the trail.

For the complete scoop on cougars, see the Mount Rainier National Park Home Page:

www.nps.gov/mora/ncrd/cougar.htm

For bears, see the U.S. Scouting Service Project Page:

www.usscouts.org/safety/safe_bea.html

For tick information, see the USDA Web Page:

www.fda.gov/fdac/features/1999/lymeside.html

For yellow jacket information, see the Health Central Web Page:

www.healthcentralsympatico.com/mhc/top/000033.cfm

Snow trail across Corral Pass (Run 24)

WEATHER

Heat: Extreme heat is not usually a problem in Western Washington, but there is the occasional heat wave, even in March or late October. And temperatures in Eastern Washington can easily top 90 or 100 degrees in the summer. The most important thing is to stay hydrated. If you are sweating a lot, water alone is not enough. Drink electrolyte replacement fluids or take electrolyte tablets. I usually carry a two-water-bottle pack, one bottle with an electrolyte drink and the other with water. For long runs, I carry additional electrolyte drink mix or use electrolyte replacement capsules. I take one capsule every two hours. Some of my sweatier friends take one or more per hour. Experiment while training to find the optimal electrolyte solution for you.

Cold: In the Northwest, it's more common to encounter colder than expected weather, even in the middle of summer. Temperatures can change quickly in the mountains. It can be a perfectly lovely day in Seattle, yet a nasty cloud will move in on the mountains bringing with it high winds, precipitation, and a quick drop in temperature. The temperature lowers with elevation gain, as does protection from the sun. Remember that the mountains create their own weather. Plan for it to be considerably colder at the top of the mountain. Use sunscreen when needed.

Snow can be fun to run in. A coat of sparkling white on the wet, dark forest or rolling, sage-covered hills is refreshing. If the snow is a few days old, you can see the tracks of every animal in the area. Unfortunately, if it is snowing, you often cannot see the trail. It can get quite disorienting when everything is white. A compass and a map can help you find your way back to the trail, especially if you pay attention to where you have been. Use an altimeter and a topographic map to help establish your position. Your old familiar stomping grounds can look completely different in the snow. Don't take risks by thinking you know the area too well to get lost.

Thunderstorms: Thunderstorms are less frequent in the Northwest than in other parts of the country, but they can move in quickly, almost without warning. The weather forecast should be your first warning, but Northwest runners still head out to run even when they know thunderstorms are possible. Dark, threatening clouds or the distant sound of thunder may warn you that a thunderstorm is on its way. I had never worried about lightning strikes until I was pacing a friend in the Wasatch Front, an annual 100-mile race in Utah. The night before the race we watched lightning dance across the mountaintops. I asked some race participants what to do in case of lightning. The response was "Don't be the tallest thing around." This is much easier in the forests of Western Washington than on the bare rock of Utah. However, you can find yourself quite exposed in Eastern Washington. The Federal Emergency Management Agency (FEMA) offers the following suggestions for keeping yourself safe in the event of lightning.

- Attempt to get into a building or car.
- If no structure is available, get to an open space and squat low to the ground as quickly as possible. If in the woods, find an area protected by a clump of trees—never stand underneath a single large tree in the open. Be aware of the potential for flooding in low-lying areas.
- Crouch with hands on knees.
- Avoid tall structures such as towers, tall trees, fences, telephone lines, or powerlines.
- Stay away from natural lightning rods such as golf clubs, tractors, fishing rods, bicycles, or camping equipment.
- Stay away from rivers, lakes, or other bodies of water.
- If you are isolated in a level field or prairie and you feel your hair stand on end (which indicates that lightning is about to strike), bend forward, putting your hands on your knees. A position with feet together and crouching while removing all metal objects is recommended. Do not lie flat on the ground.

Hail often accompanies thunderstorms in the mountains. The Northwest rarely sees hail the size of golf balls as reported in other parts of the country, but our smaller hail comes down with force and can really irritate a bare head. Keep a hat in your running pack.

Always bring plenty of food, water, and clothing for the time and conditions you expect. For the unexpected, it's a good idea to have a garbage bag tucked away in your pack. You can use it as a tarp or to wrap around yourself to keep warm. It's also wise to carry an extra energy bar in the pack to keep you going until help arrives. I have gloves, a small LED light, and a Tyvek® jacket that live in my pack. They've come in handy many times during unpredictable Northwest summers.

TRAIL ETIQUETTE

Do not chase or feed wildlife. Do not take or trample vegetation. Stay on trails or hard-packed surfaces so that you do not add to erosion problems. Be courteous to hikers. Thank them when they move to the side of the trail for you and try to let them know when you're coming up behind them. It is common to say "passing on the left" or whichever side it makes more sense to pass on. You don't want to give hikers reasons to dislike trail runners by forcing them out on a dangerous precipice to let you go by. If the trail is single track and you can't get by without the person moving off the trail, say something like, "I'd like to pass when you find a safe place to let me by." On all trails, horses have the right of way. Move to the side of the trail until they pass. It makes sense to yield right of way to fast downhill traffic since they may be unable to stop.

Do not litter! Carry out all of your trash. Those little power gel packets and string cheese wrappers do not make for a beautiful environment. To keep the water supply pure, move away from trails and streams to take care of bodily functions. Dig pit toilets, use biodegradable toilet tissue, or pack it out. If you like to bring your canine friends on trail runs, follow the rules for dogs posted at the trailhead. Pack out their leavings too.

HOW TO USE THIS BOOK

Each trail description opens with a list of quick information including the difficulty of the course, the course geometry, the approximate time and distance required to complete the route, and how much water you'll need to carry. Elevations are given, and runners are advised to check the freezing level and weather forecasts to determine

Wildflowers line the trail from Hurricane Hill (Run 2).

whether there is snow on the trails at elevations above 2000 feet in the winter. Additional information includes the best season for running the trail, whether permits are required, and suggested maps. Check the appendix for an at-a-glance chart listing the specifications for each trail.

Difficulty Rating: The trails in this guide are rated as Easy, Moderate, and Strenuous. Easy trails may include some hills that the new trail runner might prefer to walk, but there should be few obstacles on the trail. Footing is good and an experienced trail runner can run the entire course. An example is Point Defiance Park (Run 42) in Tacoma.

Moderate trails are a mix of easy and challenging sections. The more challenging or technical trails require speed control to avert collisions with objects such as boulders or trees and careful foot placement to avoid tripping over roots, rocks, and logs. An example is Wallace Falls (Run 15) in the North Cascades.

The most strenuous trails feature considerable elevation gain and loss, tricky footing, and many obstacles. You may find yourself skidding down scree-covered paths, dodging trees on steep downhills, and using your hands to climb up. An example is the Chuckanut Mountain (Run 4) near Bellingham.

Distance and Time Calculations: As many Northwest trail runners participate in races covering more than 30 miles (ultra marathons), several scenic and challenging routes of 20 to 35 miles are included in this guide. For routes over 12 miles, an alternate shorter loop or satisfying turnaround point is included.

The distance and the approximate time it will take to cover a route are listed in each header. The running times are based on my pace, including stopping to take pictures and consult maps. On an out-and-back course with considerable elevation gain, assume a 4-miles-per-hour or a 15-minute-mile pace averaged over the course distance. In determining distances, I used Department of Natural Resources (DNR), United States Geological Survey (USGS) and Green Trails Maps, and existing trail guides. I also checked the mileage against the time it takes to run the course, but distances may not be exact. Different maps for the same area often give different distances for the same trail segment.

Elevation Profiles: Data for the elevation profiles was collected once per minute, so some hills of less than 0.1 mile may not be reflected.

Course Geometry: The routes are described with three geometries. Point-to-point usually involves two cars, such as Kachess Lake to Snoqualmie Pass. A loop route returns to the same place it started, but for the most part, will not cover the same ground. An example is the

Lynne Werner, happy to have arrived at Blue Lake (Run 10)

Bridle Trails State Park. An out-and-back trail goes in one direction to a certain destination then follows the same route back to the starting point. Dosewallips to Gray Wolf Pass is an out-and-back run. For the trails that are combinations, the predominant type will be listed in the heading.

WATER

The amount of water required for each trail is given in ounces. By running these trails in different seasons, I've come up with a conservative estimate for the amount of water needed on the course. If it is hotter than normal or if you tend to perspire profusely, bring more water. Whenever there are streams or springs on the trail for emergency water, they are noted. The emergency water sources should be treated as that and precautions should be made for bacteria and parasites. See the Nutrition and Hydration section for details on water filters and iodine tablets.

HAVE FUN!

Trail runners are a great group of people. Understand your limits. Prepare for anything and everything, and go out there with your friends and be kids again.

A NOTE ABOUT SAFETY

Safety is an important concern in all outdoor activities. No guidebook can alert you to every hazard or anticipate the limitations of every reader. Therefore, the descriptions of roads, trails, routes, and natural features in this book are not representations that a particular place or excursion will be safe for your party. When you follow any of the routes described in this book, you assume responsibility for your own safety. Under normal conditions, such excursions require the usual attention to traffic, road and trail conditions, weather, terrain, the capabilities of your party, and other factors. Because many of the lands in this book are subject to development and/or change of ownership, conditions may have changed since this book was written that make your use of some of these routes unwise. Always check for current conditions, obey posted private property signs, and avoid confrontations with property owners or managers. Keeping informed on current conditions and exercising common sense are the keys to a safe, enjoyable outing.

The Mountaineers Books

OLYMPIC PENINSULA

The majestic Olympic Mountains rise from sea level to 7969 feet in elevation for Mount Olympus, the highest of the peaks. This nearly 6000-foot ridge forms the first line of defense against the precipitation-laden clouds bearing in from the Pacific Ocean. The western edge of Olympic National Park receives the most rainfall with an average of more than 145 inches per year, but the lower portions of the Hoh, Queets, and Quinault Rivers are also designated as park rain forests.

The diverse climatic zones and the ever-present moisture support a lush forest and animal life. Within the park, seven different trees have been classified as "World's Largest" for their type. The park is filled with well-marked trails, many of which can be run year-round.

Europeans sailed along the coast of the Olympic Peninsula in the eighteenth century, but the interior wasn't explored until 1885. Early visitors were quick to advocate protection of this pristine ecological area. President Cleveland designated it as a Forest Reserve in 1897, Theodore Roosevelt initiated National Monument status in 1909, but it wasn't until 1938 that Franklin D. Roosevelt signed the legislation creating the Olympic National Park.

1 QUINAULT LOOP

Distance	4 miles
Course geometry	Loop
Running time	1.25 hours
Elevation gain	450 feet
Highest altitude	480 feet
Difficulty	Easy
Water	Not required
Restrooms	Bathroom with water at trailhead
Permits	None required
Area management	Olympic National Forest
Maps	Olympic National Forest Map, Quinault Loop Map available at Quinault Village Ranger Station
Season	Year-round

This is a great little run that you can do while your nonrunning friends and family tour the half-mile Quinault Rain Forest Nature Trail. The Quinault Rain Forest trails have fewer tourists than the better-known Hoh trails, but the lower Quinault River Valley gets 145 inches of rain per year making it a true temperate rain forest. Enjoy the lovely green curtains of moss in the old-growth forest of Western red cedars, Western hemlocks, Douglas firs, and Sitka spruce on this gently rolling trail.

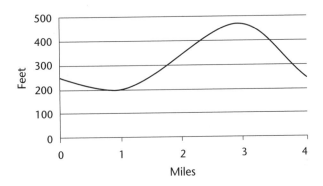

GETTING THERE

From U.S. Highway 101, 46 miles north of Hoquiam and 65 miles south of Forks, take the Lake Quinault South Shore Road. After 1.3 miles, turn into the Rain Forest Trail parking lot on the south side of the road.

Nature Trail posted map

THE RUN

Heading left from the nature trail sign, run through Willaby Campground (A) then along Lake Quinault. Little paths allow beach access from houses, but there is nothing that can be confused as another trail. The route pulls away from the waterfront on a well-maintained, well-marked trail. The trail goes by Falls Creek Campground, crosses the main road, then joins a dirt road (B). There is a sign posted here with a map of the trails. Continue right on the Loop Trail, crossing Cascade Creek and Falls Creek and eventually coming into Cedar Swamp. There are boardwalks to keep you out of the deep mud. As you move in from the lake to the forest, you enter the world of the temperate rain forest with 10-foot-tall devil's clubs, huge ferns, and club moss dripping from the trees. The trail through the forest has enough hills to give you a good workout. The hills are short, though, so you should be able to make it back to the parking lot in good time. Where the Willaby Creek Trail goes left, stay right (C). In about 1 mile you will join the Nature Trail (D) and soon be back at the trailhead.

Several trails lead off from the main trail. Each intersection is well marked, so you do not have to worry about getting lost. If you wish to do a longer run, take one or more of the loops shown on the maps posted at the trail intersections.

SIGNIFICANT TRAIL LANDMARKS

A. It is 0.3 mile to Willaby Campground; run through on road and pick up trail at north end.
B. Trail passes Falls Creek Campground, crosses road, and joins a dirt road. Go right on the Loop Trail.
C. Intersection with Willaby Creek Trail. Stay to the right.
D. The Nature Trail leads back to the trailhead.

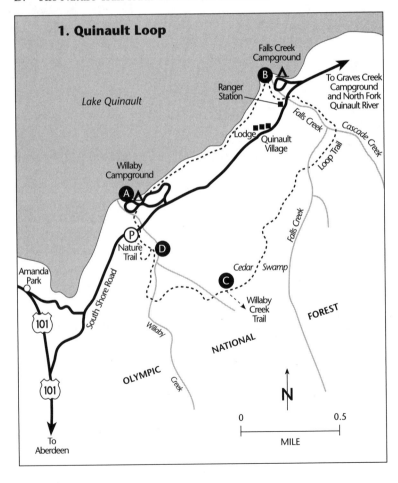

2 HURRICANE HILL TO ELWHA RANGER STATION

Distance	7.5 miles
Course geometry	Point to point
Running time	2 hours
Elevation gain	730 feet with 5300 feet of descent
Highest altitude	5757 feet
Difficulty	Moderate
Water	40 ounces
Restrooms	At ranger stations near trailheads on both ends
Permits	National park entrance fee, $10 for seven-day pass
Area management	Olympic National Park
Maps	Olympic National Park, USGS Hurricane Ridge
Season	July through October

This is a high-payoff run in many ways. The views are incredible, the trail is well maintained, and the route is almost entirely runnable. Hurricane Hill seems to be at the top of the world, putting you face to face with the highest peaks in the Olympics. You can see from Canada, just across the water to the north, to the mountain peaks of Oregon to the south, and the wildflowers bloom continuously from spring through summer. This is a trail with options for family members. The Hurricane Ridge Visitor Center has more than a mile of groomed trail. The first mile of this run is also on a paved "tourist" trail. Your family or friends can come up to Hurricane Hill with you, do the trails across from the visitor center, then meet you at the Elwha Ranger Station.

Please note that the Olympic National Forest is a wilderness and there is always the possibility of encountering bears, cougars, and other wildlife.

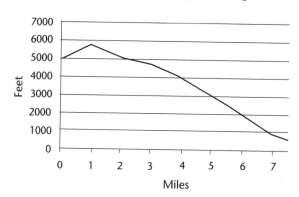

The trail to Hurricane Hill

GETTING THERE

From U.S. Highway 101 in Port Angeles go south on Hurricane Ridge Road. The Hurricane Hill trailhead is 18.6 miles from Highway 101 at the end of Hurricane Ridge Road. The visitor center at the base of the hill sells USGS maps for the entire Olympic National Park. For the Elwha Ranger Station trailhead, take Olympic Hot Springs Road from Highway 101 and go 3 miles to the Elwha Ranger Station. The trailhead is a few hundred feet up the unpaved road just past the ranger station. If you prefer lots of uphill and little down, or if you want to give your driver a little more time at the top, start here.

THE RUN

From the Hurricane Hill trailhead (A) to the summit (B), you will have paved trail and probably some company. Head up to the Hurricane Hill summit (bring your driver along for the hike this far if you're doing a point-to-point run rather than an out-and-back), then as you head back down from the summit turn right at the sign that reads ELWHA RANGER STATION 6.1 (C). From here you will see more of the panorama, more wildflowers, and more gnarly alpine vegetation, but few people. There are no signs along this trail, but no other trails branch off it.

After the first mile along the ridge, with views of the Strait of Juan de Fuca and Vancouver Island, the trail becomes a series of switchbacks through grassy meadows. The tall, fast-growing grass is the only thing obstructing a view of the trail. Continue down on the grassy switchbacks, then on switchbacks through old-growth forest. Enjoy the long, runnable downhill. In the last few miles, waterfalls and creeks occasionally cross the trail. You emerge from the trail onto an unpaved road (D). Continue down the road and turn right at the stop sign onto the paved road. The Elwha Ranger Station (E) with a bathroom and running water is a few hundred feet ahead on your right. For a 15-mile out-and-back run, I recommend starting at the Elwha Ranger Station for the long downhill finish.

SIGNIFICANT TRAIL LANDMARKS

A. Follow paved trail from the Hurricane Hill trailhead parking lot.

B. It is 1 mile to the Hurricane Hill summit.

C. Coming down from the summit, it is 1.3 miles to a junction with the Elwha Ranger Station Trail. Turn right onto this trail and follow it for 6 miles.

D. Trail merges with an unpaved road; follow it to a stop sign. Turn right onto the paved road.

E. Elwha Ranger Station.

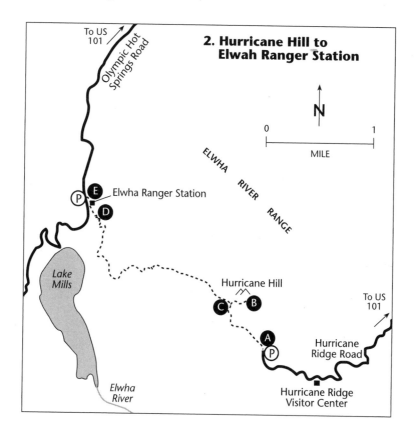

⅔ DOSEWALLIPS TO GRAY WOLF PASS

Distance	25.2 miles
Course geometry	Out and back
Running time	9 hours
Elevation gain	5940 feet
Highest altitude	6240 feet
Difficulty	Strenuous
Water	40 ounces
Restrooms	Outhouse and water at trailhead
Permits	Overnight use only requires permit
Area management	Olympic National Park
Map	Olympic National Park
Season	July through October

This trail is a beautiful introduction to the magnificence of Olympic National Park. The route initially follows the deep, V-shaped canyon of the Dosewallips River, then climbs gently for 9 miles, passing through various plant zones with the sharply rising Olympic range on all sides. In the lower elevations the trail is lined with wild rhododendrons growing to great heights in the lush forest understory. This run is comfortably shaded even on the hottest summer day. As you get to higher elevations, the vista opens to a wide panorama of the national park. Although the Olympics are known for wetness, this trail stays dry and is well maintained.

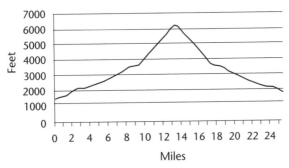

GETTING THERE

From Quilcene, travel 12 miles south on U.S. Highway 101 to Brinnon. Turn west on Dosewallips Road. Follow it 16 miles to the trailhead near the Dosewallips Campground and Dosewallips Ranger Station. The road is closed for the winter at the national park boundary approximately 2 miles east of the campground.

North from Gray Wolf Pass (toward Deer Park Trailhead)

THE RUN

From the trailhead (A) at the northwestern edge of the Dosewallips Campground (1640 feet), the trail to Hayden Pass climbs gently toward the first trail junction at 1.4 miles (B). Anderson Pass and the Enchanted Valley are to the left. Continue toward Hayden Pass. In another 1.1 miles you will reach a junction with the trail leading to Mount Constance (C). Follow the Dosewallips River and the signs to Hayden Pass.

The river is seldom in sight after the first few miles, though it can always be heard in the steep, narrow canyon below. Here, the wild rhododendrons reach high through the dense vegetation for sunlight. There are numerous creek crossings, many with bridges and some that require a "skip and a jump" to clear. Almost every creek has a signpost and a name. Appealing waterfalls greet you at creek crossings along this runnable section of trail. For a shorter run, choose one of the many waterfalls for an intermediate destination point. Deception Creek and a camp area for staging backcountry horse trips appear near the trail at approximately 8 miles (D).

At 9.2 miles you arrive at a junction of the trails to Hayden Pass and Gray Wolf Pass (E). Turn right and begin a 3.4-mile ascent to Gray Wolf Pass. The first view on the climb is back toward Wellesley Peak. The trail loops east for a mile before starting up tight switchbacks leading to the pass. Nearing your destination, you might find yourself playing a game of "where is the pass?" The trail proceeds in one direction and just when you think you see the pass, it reverses direction. The high point is above the tree line. Gray Wolf Pass (F) is at 6240 feet with spectacular views in all directions. Snow-covered Mount Olympus, the highest Olympic Mountain peak, is to the west. The view to the north looks down the pass toward the Gray Wolf River as it heads toward the Strait of Juan de Fuca. After taking in the great views, head back down the way you came.

SIGNIFICANT TRAIL LANDMARKS

A. The trailhead is at the northwestern edge of the Dosewallips Campground.
B. In 1.4 miles the trail to Hayden Pass intersects with the Enchanted Valley Trail. Continue toward Hayden Pass.
C. Constance Pass Trail junction. Continue toward Hayden Pass.
D. Deception Creek is 8.1 miles from the start. Turn around here or continue past camp area.
E. Turn right onto the Gray Wolf Pass Trail.
F. Total mileage to Gray Wolf Pass is 12.6 miles.

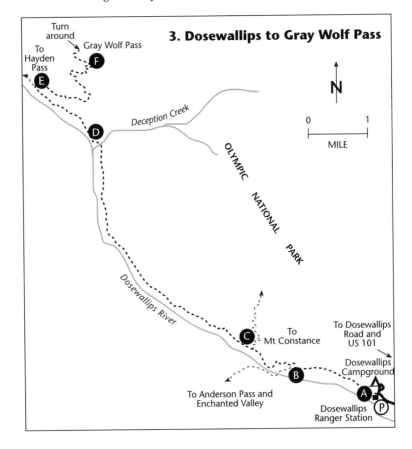

BELLINGHAM

Chuckanut Mountain, just south of Bellingham, is said to be part of the drowned range that forms the San Juan Islands. The marine shoreline of Puget Sound is on the mountain's west side, while all around it there are caves, waterfalls, wetlands, streams, and lakes, all of it accented with impressive rock specimens planted by passing glaciers.

Chuckanut Mountain, including Blanchard Hill, is sometimes called the Tiger Mountain of Bellingham. Both mountains offer the trail runner several miles of varied terrain on maintained trails. There are also parks with trail access and recreational facilities. The Chuckanut area is easily accessible from Interstate 5.

⅄ CHUCKANUT MOUNTAIN

Distance	18.5 miles
Course geometry	Loop
Running time	4.5 hours
Elevation gain	4000 feet
Highest altitude	1940 feet
Difficulty	Strenuous
Water	40 ounces
Restrooms	Toilets but no potable water at trailhead
Permits	None required
Area management	Larrabee State Park, Washington State Parks and Recreation
Map	USGS Bellingham South
Season	Year-round

The Chuckanut Mountain Trail is exceptional for its varied running conditions offering almost every kind of terrain an ultrarunner might encounter: steep ascents and descents on a dirt road, technical running along the Ridge Trail, as well as unforgettable mud slogging along the Lost Lake Trail.

Larrabee State Park surrounds this trail and consists of 2684 acres along Samish Bay to the west and the Chuckanut Mountain ridge to the east. The park is heavily wooded with beautiful fir, hemlock, and spruce trees.

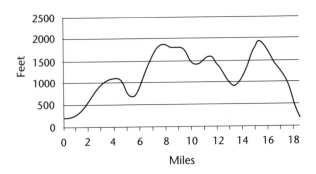

GETTING THERE

From Interstate 5, take Exit 231, then follow State Route 11 (Chuckanut Drive) 7 miles south of Bellingham to Larrabee State Park and the Clayton Beach trailhead.

THE RUN

This loop run starts at the Clayton Beach trailhead parking lot (A). (For a shorter, but still challenging, 7.6-mile loop route, park at Cyrus Gates Overlook (M) at the end of Cleator Road and start the run there.) From the trailhead, follow Fragrance Lake Road out of the parking lot, turning north and then east as you begin a long climb. The road is closed to cars. It is used for mountain biking, hiking, and running. Stay to the left at the first intersection (B) and pass a large waterfall and a dirt road as you continue your climb heading south. Fragrance Lake Trail is just a little farther and to the north.

Go through the wooden gate (C) and head to the right, running counterclockwise around the lake. Fragrance Lake was not named for the ever-present odiferous skunk cabbage, as many believe, but is derived from an early settler's name (unknown), which was regularly mispronounced by local residents. Elevation at the lake is 1000 feet.

The path around the lake has numerous footbridges and wooden walks. At the north end three-quarters of the way around the lake a small bridge crosses the outlet. Turn north after the bridge (D), climb a steep winding path to an overgrown viewpoint (elevation 1100 feet), and then take a sharp right turn down an abandoned logging spur (E). The spur heads north and generally down, sometimes steeply, to Cleator Road (F), which is 4.5 miles in.

At Cleator Road, turn right (east) and follow the dirt road up for 2.9 miles almost to the top of Chuckanut Mountain. At 0.25 mile from the top at the right-turning switchback in the road, turn to the north on the small ridge trail (G). The sign says LOST LAKE OVERLOOK. This is the most technical part of the loop and demands much attention as you work your way along. Rock surfaces on the trail can be very slippery, so use caution. Also, be sure to take in the views to the east, sometimes from 150-foot cliffs. Be careful! Avoid any side trails or game trails for the next 3 miles. You should have some clear views of civilization and Interstate 5 to the north. After these views, a minor saddle is the indicator of a sharp turn to the east and a rapid descent to a creek (H). (If you come to a gravel road and a housing development, you have gone too far.) At the bottom of the descent, cross the small creek and connect with Lost Lake Road (I).

Turn south on Lost Lake Road and head uphill on this grass-covered dirt track, which becomes a trail, a mudhole, or a stream at varying times. In the wetter seasons (most of the year here), don't worry about trying to avoid the mud and water. Just accept that you're going to get muddy and wet. The better, safer footing is usually right through

the middle of the "trail ponds," as the ground is usually level there. At the junction of the Lost Lake and Fragrance Lake Trails (J), turn right toward Fragrance Lake. A gradual climb up to the ridge crest provides some great views of Samish Bay through the trees. Continue until the long downhill levels out on a wide, dry trail. When you see a large sign saying GATE AHEAD look for a little trail back to the east (K). If you reach the white gate, you've gone 50 feet too far.

The little trail begins the last major ascent to the top of Chuckanut Mountain. This section has been dubbed "Little Chinscraper" by the folks who host the Chuckanut Mountain 50K race and developed the 18.5-mile Chuckanut Mountain Loop. Run through a heavily treed area with only occasional views back to Samish Bay, and then go up and over the Chuckanut Mountain summit (L). There are several bat caves near the top. Stay and explore or speed on down. The Cyrus Gates Overlook (M), just below the summit, is 14.9 miles into the run. On a clear day you'll have a good view of the San Juan Islands.

The next 3.6 miles are all downhill and mostly on dirt road or abandoned road sections. From the overlook, you depart on Cleator Road again near the parking area for the shorter run, almost immediately past the entrance to the ridge trail section (M). Continuing on down for about 0.75 mile, take a sharp turn to the south onto the wide, well-marked Fragrance Lake Trail (C). The trail widens more and becomes Fragrance Lake Road; this is the same road that led up from the Clayton Beach parking area at the start of the run. Go past the lake and the lake trail entrance, continuing on the road. After all the steep climbs, this long downhill is a welcome sight to the 50K racers, even with the resultant quivering quads. Two miles farther down you will be back at the Clayton Beach trailhead parking lot.

If you still crave a few more miles for the day, you can run the Interurban Trail (N) just below the parking lot. The Chuckanut Mountain 50K race starts at Fairhaven Park, which is 6.3 miles away. Adding the out-and-back Interurban Trail to the loop equals 50 kilometers (31 miles).

SIGNIFICANT TRAIL LANDMARKS
A. Trailhead behind bathrooms at Clayton Beach parking lot.
B. Stay to the left at road intersection.
C. Pass through a wooden gate and go right onto trail.
D. Three-quarters of the way around the lake cross a wooden bridge and turn right (north).

Opposite: *Chuckanut's year-round mud*

E. Take a sharp right turn onto an abandoned logging spur.
F. Cleator Road at 4.5 miles. Turn right.
G. Lost Lake Overlook. Turn left (east, then bearing north).
H. At 10.3 miles, leave ridge and turn right.
I. Go south on Lost Lake Road.
J. Turn right toward Fragrance Lake at the junction of Lost Lake and Fragrance Lake Trails.
K. GATE AHEAD sign at 14 miles. Turn right.
L. Go over the Chuckanut Mountain summit.
M. Cyrus Gates Overlook. Turn right (park here for shorter run).
N. If you want a longer run, continue on Interurban Trail.

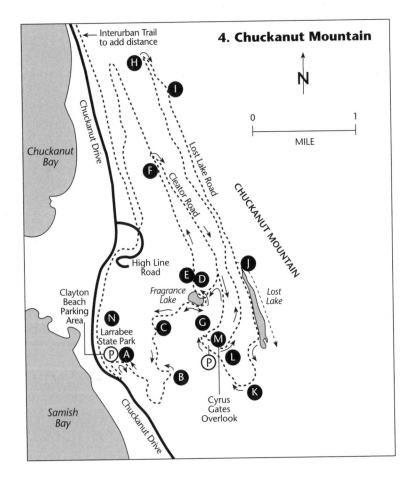

5 BLANCHARD HILL

Distance	10 miles
Course geometry	Out and back
Running time	2.75 hours
Elevation gain	1830 feet
Highest altitude	2110 feet
Difficulty	Easy to moderate
Water	40 ounces
Restrooms	Outhouse at Lizard Lake
Permits	None required
Area management	Department of Natural Resources (DNR)
Maps	USGS Bow and Bellingham South
Season	Year-round

Blanchard Hill rises from the Skagit and Samish Valleys on the southern edge of the Chuckanut Mountain ridge. The trails are well marked and maintained. With a high elevation of 2100 feet, this is a year-round trail. The terrain is hilly but not too steep or technical, making it a good trail for beginners and a fast trail for the more advanced trail runner. There are good views from the trail, second-growth forest to enjoy, and the lakes make a nice destination point. Combine this with easy access from Interstate 5 and ample parking, and it makes for a lovely half-day excursion from Seattle.

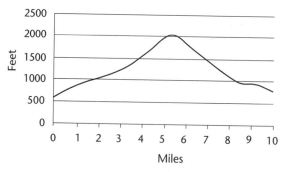

GETTING THERE

From Interstate 5 at Bellingham take Exit 240 and go west. Take the first left in 0.4 mile onto Barrel Springs Road, following signs for Blanchard Hill Trails. Turn right after 0.7 mile. There is a large parking area in 0.6 mile and the actual trail starts 500 feet beyond. Elevation here is 690 feet, and it is 5 miles to Lily and Lizard Lakes. There is a second trailhead, also with parking, 1 mile farther along the road. The lakes are 4 miles from this junction. The lower trailhead leads through a clear-cut and then turns south (left) on the road to meet the second trailhead.

THE RUN

From the first parking lot (A), head south down the road a short distance. The trail entrance is on the right with a sign noting LIZARD LAKE, LILY LAKE 5 MILES. The trail goes up a wide switchback with a nice view of Mount Baker to the east. In 1 mile the trail dumps out into another parking lot (B). Head south (left) down the road again for a few hundred feet to where a sign on the right indicates LIZARD LAKE, LILY LAKE 4 MILES. From here, the trail ascends gradually southwest with an expansive view of Samish Bay and the Skagit Valley to the south. The Olympics stand above the bay to the southwest.

View over Samish Bay from the Pacific Northwest Trail

The trail then jogs back to the northeast and comes to a junction with the Pacific Northwest Trail (PNT) (C). Pass this trail and continue up and to the right. Follow the now wooded trail up until you reach the high point and a T intersection (D) with a sign for LILY LAKE 0.1 MILE, LIZARD LAKE 0.4 MILE. Choose your lake, it's easy to go to both. Take in Lily Lake, then double back to Lizard Lake. There is an outhouse at Lizard Lake. The lakes are small with lots of snags and fallen trees in them. Not the most scenic places, but a good destination for a nice day's run. Go back to the intersection and head down the way you came. The trail is nicely maintained and if there aren't too many bikes, you can make a safe, rapid descent.

SIGNIFICANT TRAIL LANDMARKS

A. First parking lot. Trail entrance is to the right a short distance down the road.

B. Second parking lot and trailhead at 1 mile. Go left, then right onto trail to Lizard and Lily Lakes.

C. Intersection with Pacific Northwest Trail at 2.9 miles. Stay on lakes trail, continuing uphill and to the right.

D. High point at T intersection. Lily Lake is left, Lizard Lake is right. Visit lakes and return the way you came.

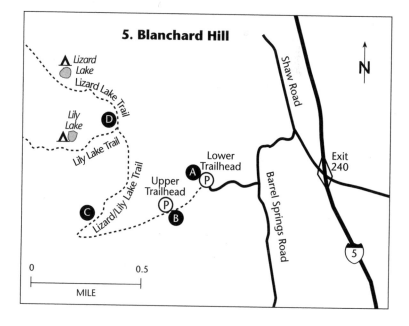

6 OYSTER DOME

Distance	8 miles
Course geometry	Loop
Running time	3 hours
Elevation gain	3000 feet
Highest altitude	2120 feet
Difficulty	Moderate to strenuous
Water	40 ounces
Restrooms	No
Permits	None required
Area management	Department of Natural Resources (DNR)
Maps	USGS Bellingham South, DNR Chuckanut
Season	Year-round

The Oyster Dome loop offers the runner an easily accessible workout on forested hills with incredible views any time of year. Samish Bay, the San Juan Islands, and the Olympic Peninsula are well presented within 1000 feet of climbing.

The run starts and ends on the Pacific Northwest Trail (labeled PNT on the signs). When completed, this trail will extend from Washington's west coast well into Montana. It's unclear how the trail will cross Puget Sound, but you can't go much farther west on this part of the trail without falling into Samish Bay.

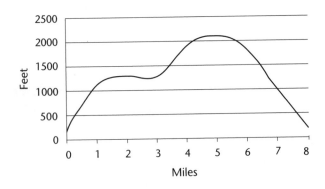

GETTING THERE

From Interstate 5, take Exit 231 (Chuckanut Drive/State Route 11). Drive north on State Route 11 to milepost 10; park on the wide left shoulder. Cross the road to the PNT trailhead.

THE RUN

The Pacific Northwest Trail (PNT) comes right down to Chuckanut Drive near milepost 10 (A). Enter the trail and ascend the large switchbacks 1.6 miles to Samish Overlook (B), cross the dirt road, and re-enter the trail marked PNT. After going north for a short distance, the trail heads east until the 2.8-mile point where it is marked as Max's Shortcut (C). The DNR map refers to this section as the PNT as well, and all the trails mentioned here have PNT at the top or bottom of the signs. The trails are muddy in places, but the wetness is what keeps our forests green. Follow this trail mostly north. There are places where the horse trail and the hiking trail split. This is to keep horses off the wooden footbridges. The trails generally merge after the water crossings.

When you come to Lily Lake (D), turn left. The lake is a little added bonus on the Oyster Dome route (see the Blanchard Hill route for an extension of the Lily Lake Trail). The trail signs and maps are a little unclear on what they want to call this segment of trail, but follow signs that point toward Oyster Dome. The dome itself, a rocky outcropping, is up a scant quarter-mile spur trail. There is a sign that says OYSTER DOME (E). Run out to the dome, crossing Lily Creek, then return to this

Samish Bay, Doug Beyerlein, and the Pacific Northwest Trail

sign, turn right, and go down the hill. The next 2-mile segment is mostly comprised of fairly technical downhill. I like to run this to practice foot placement and speed while keeping my balance. Others might prefer to run this loop trail in reverse to do this part as uphill, where the terrain appears more as a series of rock and root steps. The trail returns to the smoother downhill once it intersects with the PNT (F). This portion of the PNT should look familiar, as it is the trail you started on. You'll begin to glimpse the highway below and maybe even see your car. It's a nice end to a challenging run.

SIGNIFICANT TRAIL LANDMARKS

A. Enter trail near Chuckanut Drive milepost 10.
B. It is 1.6 miles to the Samish Overlook. Cross the dirt road and pick up the trail downhill and to the left.
C. Max's Shortcut is at 2.8 miles. Turn left onto this trail.
D. Lily Lake. Go left, following sign to Oyster Dome.
E. Spur trail to Oyster Dome. Run out to the dome and return to this point to pick up the trail.
F. An intersection with the segment of the PNT that ends on Chuckanut Drive. Follow PNT downhill to starting point.

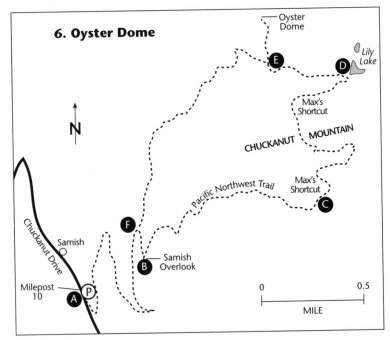

7 SQUIRES LAKE

Distance	5 miles
Course geometry	Loop
Running time	1.5 hours
Elevation gain	700 feet
Highest altitude	900 feet
Difficulty	Easy
Water	Optional
Restrooms	Outhouse at trailhead
Permits	None required
Area management	Whatcom County and Skagit County Parks and Recreation Departments
Map	Best map is posted at the trailhead
Season	Year-round

Squires Lake Park is a little gem that is close to Interstate 405. It is easy to find and has well-maintained, well-marked trails. The trails pass by the lake and beaver ponds and run along the ridge. From the ridge, the vista opens onto Lake Samish to the north and Skagit Valley to the south.

The sign at the park entrance informs that "Squires Lake Park was created in 1995 through the efforts of the Whatcom Land Trust and generous private contributions. Local businesses and individuals constructed the dam, built the parking lot, and paid for initial development and park management. An anonymous gift of $3,000,000 matched Whatcom County Conservation Futures money to buy the property. Squires Lake is now protected by a conservation easement held by the Land Trust. A product of community cooperation, this park is for you to enjoy and respect."

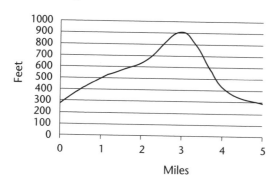

Squires Lake Vista and Ridge Trail

Preserving the natural environment for our children's children is a nice gesture that has been occurring more and more in Washington state. It's a trend that lends hope to the future.

GETTING THERE

From Interstate 5 just north of the Blanchard Hill Trail exit, take Exit 242, Nulle Road, and head east. Nulle Road joins Old Highway 99 North in a scant half mile. There is a sign for Squires Lake Parking. The one-way entrance is on the left.

THE RUN

Head north from the parking lot up the 0.3-mile, switchback trail to a small bridge and lake overlook (A). Go left and run clockwise around the lake until you come to a trail junction (B). For the first pass, go left at the junction, then right on a small, unpaved road (C). (The trail purist who refuses to run on road can leave out this section and instead continue right at B on the trail to the beaver pond for a 4-mile run.) The gravel road goes along the north side of the main beaver pond. Soon you come to a PRIVATE sign. Turn around and return to the trail marked Beaver Pond Loop (D). The pond really was built by beavers, as evidenced by sharp teeth marks on the trees in the vicinity. In addition to beavers, hawks and eagles frequent the pond.

When you finish the beaver pond loop, pick up the Squires Lake Loop Trail. To do the whole loop you may have to do the beaver pond loop 1.5 times to reach the Squires Lake Loop Trail. There are two junctions to this trail from the beaver pond loop. It doesn't matter which one you take, as they both arrive at the same place. On the Squires Lake Loop Trail you will see a sign for South Ridge Trail (E). When you complete the Squires Lake Loop Trail, head up the South Ridge Trail for a nice view of Lake Samish. On the ridge there is a sign indicating the park boundary. Beyond this is a little more ridge trail with a very steep drop-off on the right, then a clear-cut area that offers views of Skagit Valley to the south and, on a clear day, Mount Rainier and the Olympics to the west. Double back on the South Ridge Trail, staying to the left at trail intersections. At the north end of the lake near the small bridge (A) go left down the switchbacks to the parking lot.

SIGNIFICANT TRAIL LANDMARKS

A. 0.3 mile to Squires Lake. Run clockwise around the lake.

B. A junction with a gravel road at 0.5 mile. Turn left onto the road to reach the north side of the beaver ponds.

C. Turn right at the trail junction at 0.7 mile.

D. Start of the Beaver Pond Loop Trail. Go left or right; either way you come out on the Squires Lake Loop Trail.

E. The South Ridge Trail begins at 3.6 miles. Go up to the ridge. Turn left at (A) and follow the switchbacks out.

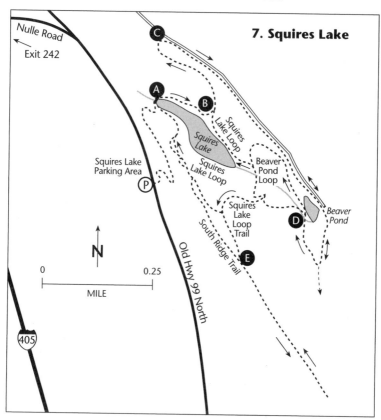

NORTH CASCADES

The North Cascades have a rugged beauty all their own. Steep rock walls surround deep lush valleys. The trails included in this section can be accessed from State Route 20, U.S. Highway 2, and the Mountain Loop Highway. Although these trails are a bit of a drive for most people, the region is a beautiful alternative to Mount Rainier and the Central Cascades. The Pacific Crest Trail traverses the North Cascades at Rainy Pass, and this section has an entirely different feel from the segment near Snoqualmie Pass.

8 BAKER LAKE

Distance	26 miles
Course geometry	Out and back
Running time	7 hours
Elevation gain	2540 feet
Highest altitude	990 feet
Difficulty	Moderate
Water	40 ounces
Restrooms	No toilets or potable water available at trailhead, toilets at 13 miles
Permits	Northwest Forest Pass required
Area management	North Cascades National Park/Mount Baker Ranger District
Maps	Green Trails #46, USGS Welker Peak
Season	Year-round

This trail is just beautiful. If you take a camera, don't use up your film too early, because it keeps getting better! Baker Lake is a good intermediate trail with many short ups and downs. Well maintained and well marked, this trail is not the usual "flat run along the lake." Instead, it undulates continuously along the eastern shore. Baker Lake is 10 miles long and nestled along Mount Baker's east side at an elevation of 722 feet. The area features some of the largest fir and cedar stands in the Northwest. Baker Lake receives 120 inches of rainfall per year. The huge trees, various fungi, and long hanging mosses of the temperate rain forest add to the beauty of this trail.

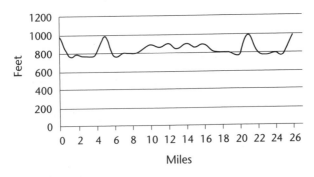

GETTING THERE

From Interstate 5 north of Mount Vernon take Exit 230 (Burlington). Follow State Route 20 (North Cascades Highway) to milepost 82 (23

East Baker Lake Trail and Ian Gillis

miles from Interstate 5). Go left on Baker Lake–Grandy Road. In 14 miles, turn right on Forest Service Road 1106 and drive through the Baker Lake–Komo Kulshan Campground. In approximately 1 mile turn right over the Upper Baker Dam. Quite a prelude to a trail, the narrow single lane across the dam has water on the left and a 200-foot drop on the right. Turn left on Forest Service Road 1107. The trailhead is 0.7 mile farther on the left.

THE RUN

The east Baker Lake trailhead is at 970 feet on the lake's south end (A). There is another trailhead and parking lot at the north end. The northbound trail, which quickly drops 100 feet, starts out quite wide and is very runnable through dense forest. It has spectacular vistas of Mount Baker's beautiful east side, a lesser known aspect since the mountain is generally seen from the Interstate 5 corridor on the west.

In 1.8 miles there is a side trail to a campsite near Anderson Point (B). Continue past the campground trail. Two miles farther is the Maple Grove Campground (C). There is one last view of the mountain before it goes out of sight as you follow the lake northeastward. The trail rolls up and down all through this area. You get a good workout, but since the down quickly balances the up, it seems deceptively easy. The lake and the mountain are always in view through the trees. At about 6.5 miles, the shoreline takes a turn to the east. Soon the trail bends around a beautiful cove formed by Noisy Creek (D). This is a good place to replenish water, though there are many creeks along the trail (always treat water taken from natural sources). The Noisy Creek Campsite and Bridge are here. Just beyond, there are some of the largest fir and cedar trees in the Northwest. The moss drips from the trees and seems to cover everything on the ground as well. From this, you might expect everything to be wet, but the trail is generally dry.

As you leave the lake, the trail drops down to the level of the Baker River and runs through a brushy area (E). The sandy river rock terrain indicates that this was the riverbed before the present channel was formed. At 12 miles, a metal bridge crosses the river. It is 0.8 mile to the north end trailhead and parking lot (F). You can run Forest Service Road 11 to Forest Service Road 1106 and back to the south trailhead, making a full loop of the lake, but 4 miles of dusty road and about 8 miles of pavement are less enjoyable than turning around and further savoring the lush forest on the return trip. Of course, for a shorter run you can turn back wherever you want. A spectacular view of Mount Baker across the lake appears early—you won't miss it even on a short run. Another option is to park a car at each end and do this trail as a 13-mile point-to-point run.

SIGNIFICANT TRAIL LANDMARKS

A. Trailhead parking.
B. It is 1.8 miles from the southern trailhead to the Anderson Point Campsite. Go right.
C. Continue 2 more miles to Maple Grove Campground.
D. The Noisy Creek Bridge and Campsite is at 8.8 miles. Continue north on trail.
E. Come to a sandy, rocky trail, then a bridge crossing the river.
F. The north end trailhead and parking lot. Turn around or continue on road around the lake's west shore. To take the road, follow Forest Service Road 11 to Forest Service Road 1106 across the dam to the trailhead.

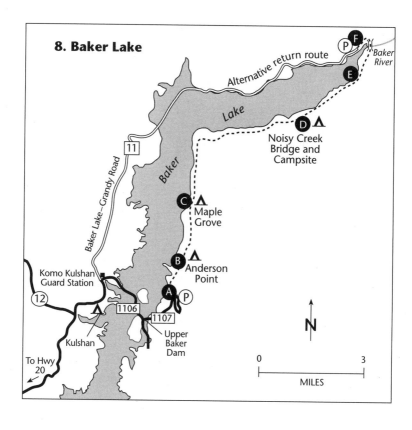

9 SAUK MOUNTAIN

Distance	7.2 miles
Course geometry	Out and back
Running time	2.5 hours
Elevation gain	2400 feet
Highest altitude	5324 feet
Difficulty	Easy to moderate
Water	40 ounces
Restrooms	Toilet but no potable water available at trailhead
Permits	Northwest Forest Pass required
Area management	North Cascades National Park/Mount Baker Ranger District
Maps	Green Trails #46, Lake Shannon, USGS Sauk
Season	July through October

This is an entirely runnable trail on switchbacks that travel mostly through meadows but with a couple of turns in second-growth forest. It's a great beginner trail, as well as a good workout for the more advanced runner wishing to sustain speed on inclines.

The summit used to have a fire lookout, but it fell into disrepair and was burned by the Forest Service about 15 years ago. Views of Mount Baker and Mount Shuksan to the north, as well as Glacier Peak and Pugh, Whitehorse, and White Chuck Mountains to the south, are better than any I've seen. On crystal clear days, you can see Mount Rainier and the San Juan Islands. On a clear day in early October, I could see the new snowline on the Cascades. Off in the distance, the Olympics were visible.

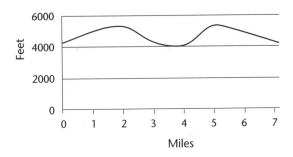

GETTING THERE

From Interstate 5 north of Mount Vernon, take Exit 230 (Burlington). Follow State Route 20 about 30 miles east through Concrete. Go about 10 miles east of Concrete and turn left (north) onto Forest Service Road 1030 near Rockport State Park. After 7 miles, when you come to a Y in the road, turn right onto Forest Service Road 1036 and drive to the trailhead at road's end.

THE RUN

I can't imagine that anyone could get lost on this trail. You can see most of the trail from the parking lot (A). From the parking lot at 4300 feet in elevation, Trail 613 ascends quickly on switchbacks through open meadow. Wildflowers abound in early summer. Occasionally, the switchbacks turn in second-growth forest. As you climb the switchbacks—at least thirty of them—you achieve an ever-increasing view of

Sauk Lake

the Sauk, Skagit, and Cascade River Valleys. The scramble to the summit (B) is across rocks. The view from the summit is well worth conquering the rocks. I thought I had already seen the best vistas in the Northwest on previous runs, but this one may take the top honor.

From the summit you can see Sauk Lake about 1400 feet below you. Turning around at the summit results in a 4.2 mile run with 1200 feet of elevation gain. If you wish to add a 3-mile round-trip diversion, head back down the trail until you see a wood sign with an arrow pointing to the Sauk Lake Trail (C). This spur trail is a little steeper, but still runnable. For the return, climb back up to the sign and head back down the switchbacks to the parking lot.

To make a good long run out of this and avoid driving on the washboard road from State Route 20 to the Sauk Mountain trailhead, park at the bottom of the forest service road (D) and run the 7 miles to the trailhead.

SIGNIFICANT TRAIL LANDMARKS

A. Parking lot. Begin run here or at beginning of Forest Service Road 1030 (see D).

B. The summit lookout is at 2.1 miles. Turn around here or continue to Sauk Lake.

C. Entrance to Sauk Lake Trail. Sauk Lake is at 3.6 miles. Turn around and go back the way you came.

D. Begin run on Forest Service Road 1030 to add 14 miles.

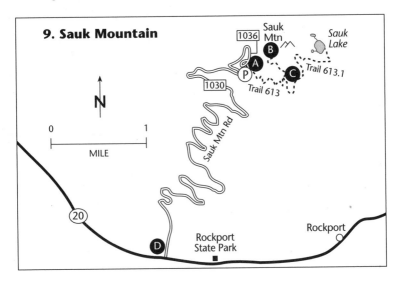

10 BLUE LAKE

Distance	4.6 miles
Course geometry	Out and Back
Running time	1.5 hours
Elevation gain	800 feet
Highest altitude	6100 feet
Difficulty	Easy
Water	40 ounces
Restrooms	Outhouse at trailhead
Permits	Northwest Forest Pass required
Area management	Okanogan National Forest
Maps	North Cascades National Park, USGS Washington Pass
Season	July through October

Blue Lake is a lovely destination for a cool run on a hot day. The trail is easily accessible from State Route 20 and provides a nice break if you're doing a long drive across the mountains.

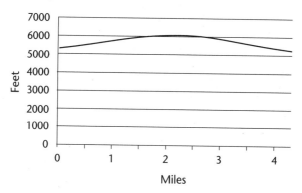

GETTING THERE

From State Route 20, 54 miles east of Marblemount or 39 miles west of Winthrop, turn south into the Blue Lake parking area. The trail starts behind the outhouse on the east side of the parking lot.

THE RUN

This is a nice, gradual, uphill run on the way in and runnable downhill on the way out. The trail starts in a silver fir forest (A) and passes some wildflower meadows before it begins to go up. On the ascent, the surrounding scenery reveals itself. Cutthroat Peak and the craggy peaks

Blue Lake

of Whistler Mountain jut out to the west, and just above you on the trail are the cliffs of Liberty Bell and Early Winters Spires. About 1.7 miles into the trail (B), another trail heads to the left through a boulder field. Ignore this and continue on toward Blue Lake. There is an old cabin as you approach the lake (C) and cool clear water in case you need a little dip.

Return the way you came, enjoying the easy grade of the well-maintained Blue Lake Trail. I hear the fishing is good, but can't vouch for it myself.

SIGNIFICANT TRAIL LANDMARKS

A.   The trailhead is behind the outhouse on the east side of the parking lot.

B.   About 1.7 miles into the trail, there is a boulder field with a trail heading left. Continue straight.

C.   Blue Lake. Turn around to go back the way you came.

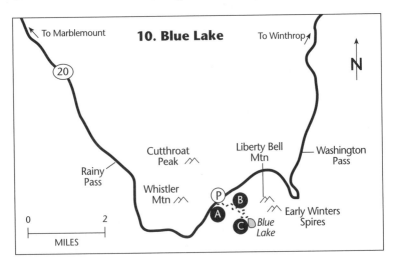

11 RAINY PASS TO CUTTHROAT LAKE

Distance	18 miles
Course geometry	Out and back
Running time	5.5 hours
Elevation gain	3700 feet
Highest altitude	6800 feet
Difficulty	Moderate to strenuous
Water	60 ounces
Restrooms	Outhouse at trailhead
Permits	None required
Area management	North Cascades National Park
Maps	North Cascades National Park, Green Trails #50, USGS Washington Pass
Season	July through October

This is a lovely, invigorating run in the summer. The area is much cooler than the parched Methow Valley (Run 12), with good climbs, well-marked trails, and breathtaking scenery. In the fall the autumn leaves add dashes of color to the stark landscape of the higher elevations. The climbs are challenging, but most of the trail is runnable. Some tricky footing on rocks between Cutthroat Pass and Cutthroat Lake prevents going fast through this area.

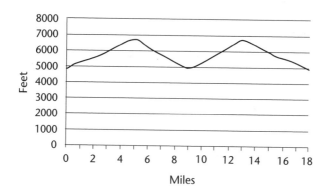

GETTING THERE

Take State Route 20 to Rainy Pass, which is about 50 miles east of Marblemount and 43 miles west of Winthrop. Park in the lot on the north side of State Route 20.

THE RUN

The run starts at Rainy Pass (elevation 4840 feet) on the Pacific
Crest Trail (A), which passes through forest with a gradual climb. Cross
the small stream and enjoy the little waterfall above. After about a mile,
the trees begin to thin and the trail gets steeper. As you continue climbing, the soil becomes more like fine crushed rock and the trees take on
the rugged alpine look of many snowy, windy winters. The trail is high
and exposed and should be avoided in bad weather. The Lyall larch
thrives in this tough environment and provides touches of beautiful
color in the early autumn. Wildflowers abound and mountain goats
occasionally wander by.

View from Cutthroat Pass

Continue on the Pacific Crest Trail to Cutthroat Pass (B) (elevation 6880 feet). From here, the surrounding peaks are at eye level. From the knoll south of the pass you can see Cutthroat Peak, the bare west slopes of Silver Star, and Liberty Bell peeking over the ridge. From this point the Pacific Crest Trail continues north to Snowy Lakes, while the running trail branches to the right. In case of emergency there is water at a campground 1 mile west of Cutthroat Pass. Go downhill from Cutthroat Pass toward Cutthroat Lake (C). The trail is signed and roughly follows Porcupine Creek. Continue down just about as far as you climbed, through meadows then cool forest, until you reach Cutthroat Lake.

If you leave a second car at the Cutthroat Campground (D), which is east of Washington Pass on Forest Service Road 400, you can continue right on Cutthroat Creek Trail to its trailhead for an 11.5-mile run. If your car is at Rainy Pass, turn around and trace your steps back over Cutthroat Pass to Rainy Pass.

SIGNIFICANT TRAIL LANDMARKS

A. Begin run at Rainy Pass on the Pacific Crest Trail.
B. Cutthroat Pass is at 5.1 miles. Continue on trail that branches to the right.
C. Cutthroat Lake is at 9 miles. Return the same way you came.
D. Cutthroat Creek Campground. Take Cutthroat Creek Trail for a longer point-to-point run.

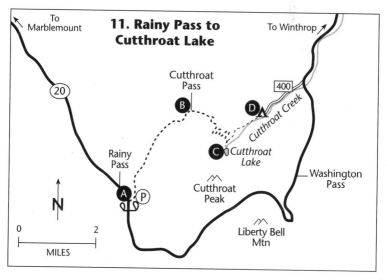

12 SUN MOUNTAIN

Distance	10 miles
Course geometry	Loop
Running time	2.5 hours
Elevation gain	900 feet
Highest altitude	2850 feet
Difficulty	Easy
Water	40 ounces
Restrooms	Outhouse at trailhead
Permits	None required
Area management	Methow Valley Sport Trails Association
Map	Methow Valley Winter Trail System
Season	May through October

This 10-mile route is entirely runnable. In the winter it is a combina-tion of cross-country skiing and snowshoe trails. It is partially shaded and at a slightly higher elevation than Winthrop, making it a little cooler than the valley for summer running.

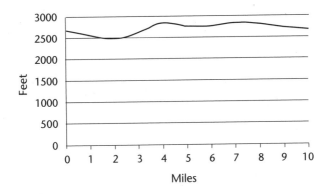

GETTING THERE
From State Route 20 immediately south of Winthrop, turn east at the end of the bridge and follow the signs for Sun Mountain Lodge. Before you get to the lodge, take the cutoff for Chickadee Trailhead.

THE RUN
The trail heads west out of the parking lot (A). Turn left onto Cabin Trail, and follow it a short way past cabins to Patterson Lake Trail (B).

Go left and follow Patterson Lake Trail for 2.6 miles as it curves along the lake. This lake is also nice for a cooling dip on a hot day. Go north through the trees on Rader Creek Trail (C), a continuation of Patterson Creek Trail, for about 1.5 miles until you see a sign for Lower Inside Passage (D). Turn right here. Lower Inside Passage opens onto Thompson Road. At Thompson Road, jut a little to the left to pick up the Overland Trail (E) headed east (right). From there, join the Criss Cross Trail (F) and go right on it over to the Yellow Jacket Trail (G), where you'll turn left.

It's not as hard as it sounds. I recommend picking up a Methow Valley Trails Association "Winter Trails" map so that you can easily see the trail names in case you find yourself on one not mentioned here. Stay on Yellow Jacket Trail until you come to the Hough Homestead, a building and stables sometimes used for group events. Turn left before the bridge and continue on Upper Fox, which is part of the Fox Loop to the north of the homestead leading to the homestead entrance, (H) to Aqualoop Trail. Run counterclockwise around Aqualoop (I), then

Patterson Lake and trail

take Lower Fox (J) south around the Hough Homestead coming out on the opposite side of the bridge. Cross the bridge, continuing to the right, then turn left on Rodeo Trail (K), which parallels Yellow Jacket Trail. At the end of Rodeo, go left onto Overland Trail (L), and then take another left onto Chickadee Trail (M), which leads you back to the parking lot. The "Winter Trails" map offers many more routes if you wish to increase your distance or add more elevation gain to your run.

SIGNIFICANT TRAIL LANDMARKS

A. Trailhead parking. Turn left onto Cabin Trail.
B. Patterson Lake Trail is at 0.3 mile. Follow it along the lake.
C. At 2.6 miles, go north on Rader Creek Trail through the trees.
D. Turn right on the Lower Inside Passage Trail at 4.6 miles.
E. At 4.7 miles, jut to the left on Thompson Road to pick up Overland Trail.
F. Go right on the Criss Cross Trail at 5.2 miles.
G. At 5.5 miles, turn left onto Yellow Jacket Trail. Continue on Yellow Jacket Trail until you come to Hough Homestead.
H. Turn left onto the Upper Fox Trail, which starts before the bridge at 6.5 miles.
I. Run counterclockwise on the Aqualoop Trail.
J. At 8.1 miles, the Lower Fox Trail goes around the homestead and comes out on the homestead side of the bridge.
K. Follow the Rodeo Trail. When it ends, go left.
L. At 9.2 miles, take the Overland Trail over to the Chickadee Trail.
M. Chickadee Trail leads back to the parking lot.

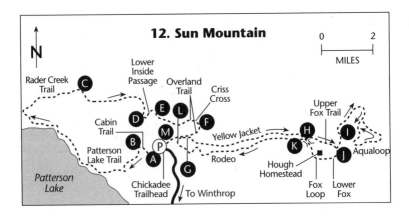

13 SUIATTLE RIVER

Distance	34 miles
Course geometry	Loop
Running time	9 hours
Elevation gain	4900 feet
Highest altitude	6000 feet
Difficulty	Strenuous
Water	60 ounces and water treatment supplies
Restrooms	Outhouse at trailhead
Permits	Northwest Forest Pass required
Area management	Mount Baker–Snoqualmie National Forest
Maps	Green Trails #112
Season	July through October

Glacier Peak's craggy pinnacle at 10,528 feet in elevation can be seen from Seattle. It is one of the big Cascade volcanoes. The area abounds with flowers and rain forest-like vegetation. Less than a mile in there are magnificent old-growth trees, nurse logs, and ferns. The views from Vista Ridge to the north include Miners Ridge, Plummer Mountain, Dome Peak, and a close-up view of Glacier Peak.

This North Cascades wilderness loop course heads southwest from the Suiattle River on the Milk Creek Trail. After 7.5 miles, it joins up with the Pacific Crest Trail (PCT) until Vista Creek at approximately 20 miles. From there, the trail follows the Suiattle River back to the start. There are a lot of steep ascents and fast, runnable descents. The views are amazing and the trail is well maintained, though not especially well marked. Water is available from several streams if you follow safe treatment procedures.

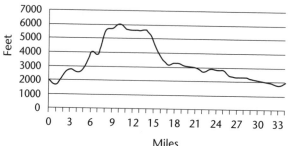

GETTING THERE

From Interstate 5 north of Everett take Exit 208 (State Route 530 East) and proceed 4 miles through Arlington then 28 miles to Darrington. Head north on State Route 530 toward Rockport. Approximately 8 miles out of Darrington there will be a Y in the road just after crossing the Sauk River Bridge. Stay to the right on Suiattle River Road. Drive the Suiattle River Road 23 miles just past the Sulfur Creek Campground to where the road ends and becomes a parking lot for the Sulfur Mountain and Suiattle River Trailheads.

THE RUN

From the parking lot, head out on Suiattle River Trail 784 (A) (elevation 1600 feet). Run 0.8 mile. At the trail junction, go right onto Milk Creek Trail 790 (B), cross over a bridge, and enter the Glacier Peak Wilderness. The trail runs through a magnificent grove of ancient and huge trees. Pass through a meadow with views of waterfalls at mile 3 (elevation 2400 feet). The trail ascends gently until mile 7.5, where you turn left to join the Pacific Crest Trail (PCT) (C) (elevation 3900 feet). There is a great view of Glacier Peak from here, and this may be used as a turnaround point.

Glacier Peak from lower Mill Creek Trail

The PCT starts in a grove of fir trees marked as STOCK AREA. This area is used as a staging area for backcountry horse packing. The entry to the PCT is not well marked, but look for it heading northwest through the grove. The trail soon leads into an area of large ferns and dense foliage. Waterfalls are to the right. After you leave this open area, you enter a large area of scree. The trail soon begins a rapid ascent on 36 switchbacks. On the constant climb you can hear the cascading water and glimpse views of the glaciers above. The crest of Milk Creek Ridge is at 11.5 miles (D) (elevation 6000 feet). Continue on the Pacific Crest Trail past a trail on the left that leads to Grassy Point (E). If you choose to go to Grassy Point (elevation 6500 feet), it is an out-and-back trail a few miles long that offers views up and down the green valley of the Suiattle River.

Continue mostly east on the PCT through meadows, streams, and possibly snow, and past Trail 798 (F) until you reach 22.7 miles (elevation 2900 feet) where there is a junction with the Suiattle River Trail 784 (G). Go left. Cross the Suiattle River on the Skyline Bridge. Cross the Miners Creek Bridge in 0.3 mile. Continue on down the Suiattle River Trail through forest and small streams that are often the tops of waterfalls. There are some really great views looking down at the waterfalls as the water plunges through the forest to the river. After 10 more miles you will be back at the bridge (B) where you crossed the Suiattle River to get on the Milk Creek Trail at the beginning of this loop. Just a little farther, 0.8 mile, is the trailhead and parking lot (A).

A late snow pack can be a problem on this trail. I have run the loop in mid-August and encountered snowfields above 5500 feet in elevation. Exercise caution in finding the trail under such conditions. A map showing elevation, an altimeter watch, and a compass facilitated my passage through the high sections of the Pacific Crest Trail.

SIGNIFICANT TRAIL LANDMARKS

A. Parking lot for Suiattle River Trail 784.

B. At 0.8 mile, take a right onto Milk Creek Trail 790.

C. At 7.5 miles, go left (east) onto Pacific Crest Trail.

D. Crest Milk Creek Ridge at 11.5 miles.

E. The Grassy Point Trail is on the left at 12.5 miles. Stay right (south) on the PCT.

F. Intersection with Trail 798 to Suiattle Pass. Go left (north) on the trail. You're at 21.5 miles.

G. Go left onto the Suiattle River Trail 784 (west).

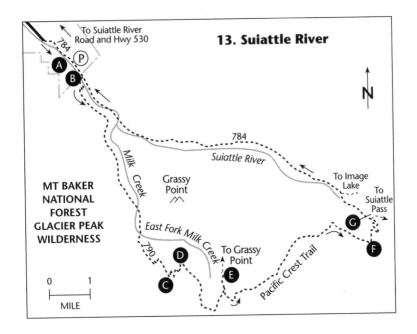

13. Suiattle River

To Suiattle River
Road and Hwy 530

784

N

784

Suiattle River

Milk Creek

Grassy
Point

MT BAKER
NATIONAL
FOREST
GLACIER PEAK
WILDERNESS

East Fork Milk Creek

790

To Image
Lake

To
Suiattle
Pass

G

F

To Grassy
Point

D

C

E

Pacific Crest Trail

0   1

MILE

14 MOUNT PILCHUCK

Distance	6 miles
Course geometry	Out and back
Running time	2.5 hours
Elevation gain	2300 feet
Highest altitude	5324 feet
Difficulty	Moderate
Water	20 ounces
Restrooms	Outhouse at trailhead
Permits	Northwest Forest Pass required
Area management	Mount Baker–Snoqualmie National Forest
Maps	Green Trails #109, USGS Verlot
Season	July through October

Mount Pilchuck offers good technical trail running experience. Most of the trail is well maintained, but boulder fields always require a little more care than dirt trail. As the trail gets steeper it also gets rockier until you are climbing on blasted granite and talus. The time allowed for this run includes waiting for your turn to climb into the lookout. It's worth it, with close-up views of Three Fingers, Whitehorse, and Shuksan Mountains, Mount Baker, Glacier Peak, and Mount Rainier. There are also spectacular views of all the cities in the Puget Sound area. Up on this lofty peak there is nothing to stop the wind, so be prepared for dramatic changes in temperature.

Mount Pilchuck is one of the few short trails in the region that reaches the summit of a major peak. The existing lookout was renovated recently and is maintained by the Everett branch of The Mountaineers. Much of the lower portion of the mountain was logged in the 1940s and 1950s, and some of the upper portion was cleared for a since-abandoned ski area within 1975-acre Mount Pilchuck State Park.

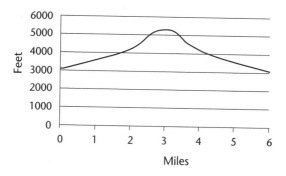

GETTING THERE

From Seattle, drive 28 miles north on Interstate 5 to Exit 194 (City Center/Stevens Pass) at Everett. Drive 6 miles east on U.S. Highway 2 to the State Route 9 exit near Snohomish. Follow State Route 9 north to State Route 92. Turn right and follow State Route 92 east 8 miles to Granite Falls. At the end of town, turn left (north) on Mountain Loop Highway. Drive 13 miles (about 1 mile past the Verlot Public Service Center) and turn right (south) on Mount Pilchuck Road (Forest Service Road 42). Drive 7 miles to the parking lot at the end of the road.

THE RUN

The trail starts in forest at 3100 feet (A). Spur trails lead off the main trail in the first few yards; going straight ahead is usually the right choice. After the forest, the trail skirts the edge of a clear-cut heading east, then switches back across the top of the abandoned ski area (B). Most of the lower portion of the trail is runnable.

Climb to the lookout

Already the views will be outstanding. Steps are built on what would otherwise be steep, slippery grades. In the rockier areas, many of the rocks are arranged into steps for an easier climb. In early October, wet rocks can have slick, icy areas. Little pikas have made their home in the talus and will watch you from the tops of rocks, seemingly without fear. The trail descends slightly to the south side of the summit before the final ascent (C). As you approach the lookout, the trail gets rockier and rockier until you are actually climbing huge boulders to get to the lookout. Climb into the lookout, where you will be protected from the wind and treated to charts naming the glorious peaks all around you. Some history of the area is provided on support beams and benches.

Be careful when running back down. Don't take shortcuts. This trail is easy to follow, but many hikers have been lost on Mount Pilchuck after they decided to explore other routes, some of which lead to very long drops onto hard rock. Be smart and safe as you treat yourself to the expansive feeling of being on the summit of this major Cascade peak.

SIGNIFICANT TRAIL LANDMARKS
A. Trailhead and parking.
B. Continue along the trail, skirting the edge of a clear-cut.
C. Begin ascent to summit.

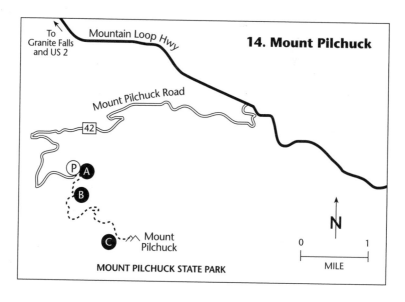

15 WALLACE FALLS

Distance	6 miles
Course geometry	Out and back or loop
Running time	2 hours
Elevation gain	1600 feet
Highest altitude	1500 feet
Difficulty	Easy to moderate
Water	40 ounces
Restrooms	Toilets and drinking fountain at trailhead
Permits	None required
Area management	Wallace Falls State Park
Maps	Green Trails #142, and map posted on board at parking lot
Season	Year-round

This is a good workout with a vertical climb and varying terrain. It is also a trail that I feel safe running alone. Descriptions of Wallace Falls boast of a "spray billowing gorge" and "earth-shaking thunder in eleven separate plunges." Though not all the plunges can be seen from the trail, there are overlooks for three spectacular ones. In the 1920s, the Wallace Falls area was the site of railroad logging. Now trees once again tower over the hillside, resulting in a dark cool forest floor covered with mosses, fern, and wildflowers. Wallace Falls State Park was dedicated in 1977.

The Woody Trail goes up 2.5 miles on switchbacks with viewpoints extending from the trail. The railroad grade, which is a favorite of families with children, is 1 mile longer, but it is less steep.

GETTING THERE
Take U.S. Highway 2 to the west end of Gold Bar and turn left (north) on First Street. Go 0.25 mile, then turn right on May Creek Road. Half a

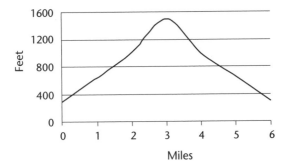

Wallace River

mile farther there is a Y in the road; stay to the left. Signs on the road lead to the Wallace Falls and Wallace Lake parking lot and picnic area.

THE RUN

From the parking lot, run 0.25 mile on a gravel trail under crackling powerlines to where the trail splits (A) at the Wallace River. From here it is 2.25 miles to the falls on the shorter but steeper Woody Trail and 3.25 miles on the longer, gentler railroad grade. Both lead to the same place. If desired, you can use the two trails to make a loop. The Woody Trail begins close to the river and goes into a gorge, then switchbacks above the stream for about a mile. The railroad grade joins the Woody Trail here (B). The united trail drops to an old bridge over the North Fork

Wallace River (650 feet in elevation). The trail ascends rather steeply and crosses a ridge to the South Fork Wallace River and onto a picnic shelter (C) (1200 feet). An overlook peers down directly over the falls and reveals the falls coming down from 250 feet up the gorge. Continue up the trail past another viewpoint with a close look at the falls. The trail ends at Valley Overlook (D), 1 mile from the North Fork Bridge. From this vantage point you can see the brink of the main falls, the Skykomish River, the towns of Gold Bar and Startup, and the Olympics.

On the way back down, when you reach the intersection of the railroad grade and the Woody Trail you have the option of a long gradual descent on the railroad grade or the steep, rock-and-root-laden plunge on the trail that is similar to those so often encountered in trail races. The trails merge at the end and head back under the crackling powerlines to the parking lot.

If you're cold after this run, the town of Gold Bar has a very warm and outstanding reptile zoo.

SIGNIFICANT TRAIL LANDMARKS

A. At 0.5 mile, the trail splits just after the powerlines. Take the right fork or Woody Trail for a steeper but shorter route; take the railroad grade, left, for a longer but less steep route.

B. The two trails merge into one for the final ascent.

C. Picnic area with waterfall views.

D. Valley Overlook turnaround.

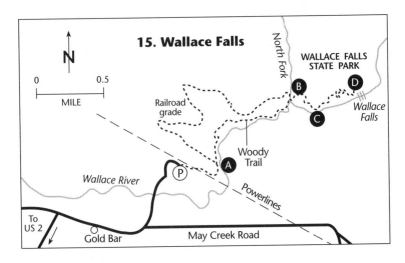

16 WALLACE LAKE

Distance	13 miles
Course geometry	Out and back
Running time	3 hours
Elevation gain	1500 feet
Highest altitude	1844 feet
Difficulty	Easy to moderate
Water	40 ounces
Restrooms	Toilets and drinking fountain at trailhead
Permits	None required
Area management	Wallace Falls State Park
Maps	Green Trails #142, USGS Wallace Lake, and map posted on board at parking lot
Season	Year-round

This wide trail is good for beginners. There are few obstacles and it is entirely runnable. The route starts on trail but goes several miles on road. Since it is a long hill up to the lake, it's also good training for the intermediate and advanced trail runners. It is 12.2 miles round trip from the parking lot to the lake outlet and another 0.5 mile to the end of the lake. The lake (elevation 1844 feet) is quite lovely and peaceful, reflecting Stickney Ridge against the sky. The trail and road up to Wallace Lake go in and out of state park property. Out of the park there is evidence of logging, but it does clear the way for some beautiful vistas.

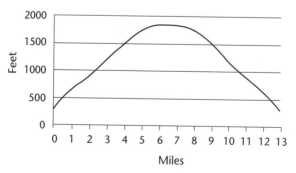

GETTING THERE
Take U.S. Highway 2 east to the west end of Gold Bar and turn left (north) on First Street. Go 0.25 mile, then turn right on May Creek Road.

Taking time to enjoy the lake

Stay left a half mile farther on when you come to a Y in the road. Signs on the road lead to the Wallace Falls and Wallace Lake parking lot and picnic area.

THE RUN

The run starts on the same trail as the Wallace Falls trip (Run 15); that is, follow the trail that leads from the parking lot and under the powerlines. Shortly after the powerlines (A), a trail to the left leads to Wallace Lake on the railroad grade. Another trail to Wallace Lake leaves the railroad grade trail on the left (B). After 1.5 miles, the trail dumps out on a road (C). Follow the road uphill almost all the way to the lake outlet. Be sure to enjoy the view on the way up to the lake, because this wide flat route can make for a thrillingly fast descent. If there is logging in progress in the area, there may be trucks on the road, but usually there is no traffic.

The road follows a stream. Even though I suspect the stream flows from Wallace Lake, my friend and I drank the water from it one very hot day after we had already gone through the 40 ounces of water we carried with us. We treated it with iodine and suffered no adverse effects from drinking out of this natural source.

At about 4 miles in on the road, just before a bridge, turn left onto a trail marked WALLACE LAKE 0.6 MILES (D). After reaching the lake outlet, you can follow the trail another 0.5 mile through old-growth forest to the end of Wallace Lake. There are cleared areas near the lake and evidence that this is a popular fishing hole. If desired, cross the inlet stream and go another mile to Jay Lake (E) (elevation 1900 feet).

From Wallace Lake you have an option of continuing on to the upper end of Wallace Falls. This route (F) is not recommended. Although it starts out relatively level and easy to follow, a logging operation has obliterated the middle portion of the trail. Beyond the logging activity, the trail traverses a very wet section where the standing water can be more than a foot deep in the winter. If the trail is ever upgraded, however, it could be quite nice.

SIGNIFICANT TRAIL LANDMARKS

A. The trail splits at 0.5 mile. Take the railroad grade to the left.
B. The trail to Wallace Lake leaves the railroad grade on the left.
C. The beginning of a road. Follow it uphill.
D. After 5.5 miles, enter the woods on the trail to Wallace Lake.
E. Continue 1 mile past the end of Wallace Lake to Jay Lake, if desired.
F. The trail route to Wallace Falls starts here.

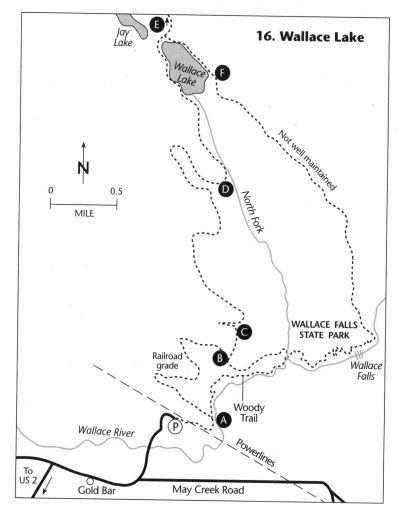

CENTRAL CASCADES

The Central Cascade Mountains are Washington's primary winter and summer playground. Interstate 90 is open year-round, as it is a major overland shipping route. Denny Creek and Pratt Lake Trails lead to many lakes in the Alpine Lakes Wilderness, and the Pacific Crest Trail is a stunning north-south route through the heart of the mountains. Less than 2 hours from Seattle, the Central Cascades provide a wilderness escape that is easy to enjoy on short day trips. Trail runners can choose from hundreds of miles of trails. This section includes a sampling of trails that demonstrate the diversity and beauty of this Northwest mountainscape.

17 MOUNT SI

Distance	8 miles
Course geometry	Out and back
Running time	2.5 hours
Elevation gain	3250 feet
Highest altitude	3900 feet
Difficulty	Moderate to strenuous
Water	40 ounces
Restrooms	Restrooms and water at trailhead
Permits	None required
Area management	Department of Natural Resources (DNR)
Map	DNR Mount Si
Season	Year-round, snow sometimes in winter

Well-maintained trails climb great switchbacks up the glacier-carved south side of Mount Si to reach stunning views at the top. The descent is somewhat technical and can be quite fast if there are not too many people and dogs on the trail. The intermediate to advanced trail runner will get a satisfying workout on this trail. Since it's an out-and-back trail, beginning runners can use this route for strengthening hill muscles, then turn around when they've had enough.

This 4167-foot, haystack-shaped mountain juts out of the virtually flat basin and can be easily identified from Interstate 90 and many parts of the Snoqualmie Valley. You can point to the craggy peak of Mount Si from Interstate 90 and say to your friends, "I ran to the top!" The mountain was named for a settler, Josiah "Uncle Si" Merritt. Mount Si has the distinction of being one of the two most-climbed mountains in Washington, the other being Mount Rainier.

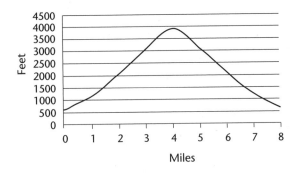

The Haystack

GETTING THERE

From Interstate 90 at North Bend, take Exit 32 (436 Avenue SE). Turn left (north) over the freeway, go 0.5 mile, and turn left onto North Bend Way. Proceed 0.25 mile, then turn right (north) onto Mount Si Road. The large trailhead parking lot is 2 miles past the bridge across the Middle Fork Snoqualmie River. Elevation at the trailhead is 650 feet.

THE RUN

There is only one trail and it has mile markers, so no directions are needed. On the way up, the trail may seem easy, though steep. Networks of tree roots form natural steps, and manmade steps lend assistance when the trail climbs over rocks near the top. The trail is wide enough to make room for hikers going in the opposite direction without jumping into the bushes. On the flat, low parts, boardwalks traverse muddy sections, and storyboards offer history and wildlife information. Sights along the way include old-growth trees slightly charred from a fire in

1909 and huge fallen "nurse" logs with hemlock roots wrapped around them and reaching into the dirt. A lovely eastern view showcases McClellan Butte in the distance. When you scramble up the final rocky portion (without climbing the Haystack), the western view includes the basin below, Mount Rainier, Lake Washington, and Seattle.

Stay in control on the descent. All those rocks and roots that formed convenient footholds for the climb up become obstacles to negotiate on the way back down. In addition, this trail's popularity may necessitate quick stops for people on the trail. If you run this trail on a weekend, start early to avoid the crowds. Although the number of people detracts from this trail, they also provide a safety net. This is one of the trails I feel comfortable running alone. Help is seldom more than a few minutes away.

Due to its closeness to Seattle, many of my ultrarunning friends use Mount Si for training repeats (charging up and down the same hill again and again). Scott Jurek, 1999, 2000, and 2001 winner of the Western States 100 Endurance Run, does repeats on Mount Si, running all the ascents and descents (during minimal hiker traffic).

SIGNIFICANT TRAIL LANDMARKS

None needed. There is only one route to the top with mile markers along the way.

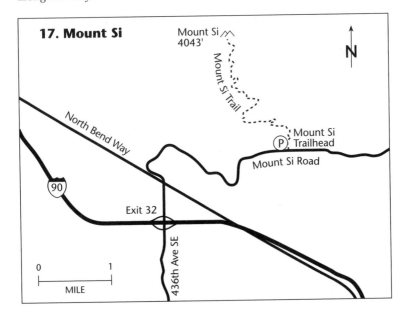

18 DENNY CREEK TO KALEETAN LAKE

Distance	19 miles
Course geometry	Out and back
Running time	8 hours
Elevation gain	6260 feet
Highest altitude	4500 feet
Difficulty	Moderate to strenuous
Water	60 ounces or means to treat water
Restrooms	Outhouse at trailhead
Permits	Northwest Forest Pass required
Area management	Mount Baker–Snoqualmie National Forest
Maps	Alpine Lakes Wilderness, Green Trails #207, USGS Snoqualmie Pass
Season	July through October

The Denny Creek Trail leads to several Alpine Lakes. The three on this route are Melakwa Lake, Lower Tuscohatchie Lake, and Kaleetan Lake. The trail climbs long switchbacks to ridges that then drop a few hundred feet to the pristine lakes. The trail is mostly runnable, with notable rocky scree exceptions. Several stunning waterfalls greet you first with their sound, then their sight, along the way. Though the upper trails may be closed from the first snow until summer, the beauty of this area makes it a must.

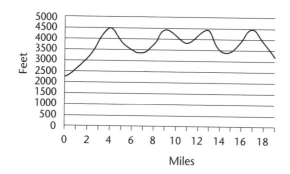

GETTING THERE

From Interstate 90 east of North Bend, take Exit 47 (Asahel Curtis/ Denny Creek). Turn left onto the overpass and proceed to a T intersection. Turn right and travel 0.25 mile to Denny Creek Road (Forest Service Road 58). Turn left and drive 2.5 miles to another left onto the briefly paved road just after the Denny Creek Campground (the paving stops after about 100 feet). The trailhead is at the end of the road.

THE RUN

The Denny Creek Trail passes under Interstate 90 at its start (A). Huge columns supporting the freeway suggest cement trees as they mix with old-growth fir of almost the same size. Denny Creek Trail goes through some rocky terrain as it passes by Keekwulee (B) and Snowshoe Falls (C), at 1.5 and 2 miles. The climb continues up for about 2000 feet to Hemlock Pass (4500 feet in elevation) (D). Melakwa Lake is a half-mile from the pass. This ends the most-traveled part of the way, and is a good turnaround point for an 8-mile outing.

To continue on from Melakwa Lake, head slightly downhill and west on Trail 1011 (E) toward Lower Tuscohatchie Lake for 3 miles. The trail can be uncomfortably overgrown here in the summer. The dense vegetation lasts for about 1.5 miles. If it's too bad, you may wish to take the loop route described below. At Lower Tuscohatchie Lake, take Trail 1010 (F) north 2.5 miles to Kaleetan Lake. Between each of the three lakes, the trail drops about 1000 feet, then climbs 1000 feet over a ridge and down a few hundred feet to the lake.

There are plenty of streams to refill water bottles. As a precaution, any water taken from these streams should be treated. The larger switchbacks on Trail 1010 provide some sustained climbs on the way out and easy running on the return. Along the way, portions of the trail appear as if the granite of the broken mountain is held together only by moss. Amazingly, white firs have found enough purchase to grow in these places. In other places, huge dead trees stand among the scree. On the ridge before Kaleetan Lake you can look west, count four mountain peaks, and see Pratt Lake. If your timing is right—late summer or early fall—the huckleberries on this trail can't be beat. To finish your run, retrace your steps past the bathing rocks of Denny Creek and back to the parking lot.

There is also a loop route option. For the loop route, don't take Trail 1010 when it branches off north toward Kaleetan Lake. Instead, head west toward Pratt Lake on Trail 1011 (F) and then pick up Trail 1007. These trails can be found on the map for Run 20, Pratt Lake. Trail 1007 winds around past Pratt and Olallie Lakes. From the Pratt Lake trailhead, proceed out to the T intersection near the Interstate 90 exit and follow Denny Creek Road 3 miles to the Denny Creek trailhead where you parked. Including the 3-mile road section, this loop is about 17 miles. If you plan ahead and have a car at each trailhead, Pratt Lake and Denny

Snowshoe Falls

Creek, it is a 14-mile route. If you include the road section and the dogleg onto Trail 1010 and Kaleetan Lake, it is 22 miles.

SIGNIFICANT TRAIL LANDMARKS

A. Denny Creek trailhead and parking.
B. Keekwulee Falls is at 1.5 miles. Continue forward.
C. It is another 0.5 mile to Snowshoe Falls. Continue forward.
D. Hemlock Pass at 4500 feet elevation. Continue toward Melakwa Lake. Turn around at Melakwa Lake for a shorter route.
E. At Trail 1011, the Lower Tuscohatchie Lake Trail, head downhill and to the left.
F. At 7 miles in, Trail 1010 goes right toward Kaleetan Lake.
G. Kaleetan Lake is the end of the trail at 9.5 miles.

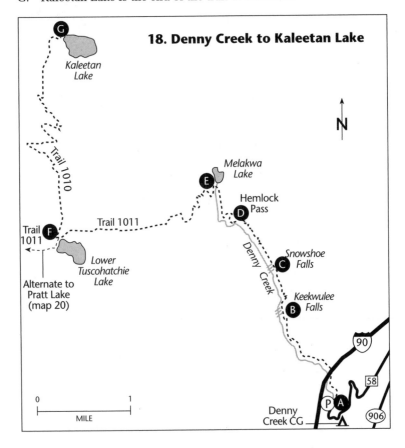

18. Denny Creek to Kaleetan Lake

19 McCLELLAN BUTTE

Distance	8.8 miles
Course geometry	Out and back
Running time	4 hours
Elevation gain	3700 feet
Highest altitude	5162 feet
Difficulty	Strenuous
Water	40 ounces
Restrooms	Outhouse at trailhead
Permits	Northwest Forest Pass required
Area management	Mount Baker–Snoqualmie National Forest
Maps	Green Trails #206, USGS Bandera
Season	July through October

As with Mount Si, this route gives you a wonderful quad workout, but with fewer people to encounter on the trail. The trail gains 3700 feet of elevation in 4.4 miles. There is a level section on the Iron Horse Trail in the first mile, and a level to slightly descending section near the butte. It's good training for continuously steep, long runs, as with some segments of the Western States 100 Endurance Run.

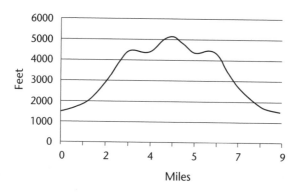

GETTING THERE

From Seattle, drive east on Interstate 90 to Exit 42 (West Tinkham Road) between North Bend and Snoqualmie Pass. Turn right from the off ramp and continue past the Department of Transportation office. The parking lot and trailhead are just past the office driveway on the right (west) side of the road.

Rocky slope of McClellan Butte

THE RUN

Trail 1015 (A) starts at 1500 feet, taking you across a bridge over Alice Creek and rising quickly through second-growth forest. At approximately 0.5 mile, you'll be out of the thick forest and on the Iron Horse Trail (B), which was the Milwaukee Railroad grade. Go right on the Iron Horse Trail, which continues to the northeast. This route takes a left on Trail 1015 (C) to head southwest toward McClellan Butte. The climb gets steeper as you proceed parallel to Alice Creek. Early in the season, snow lingers in the steep avalanche chutes crossed by the trail. Be careful crossing these slick patches, and watch for melting snow bridges on the return trip.

At about 3 miles the trail opens to a view of the south ridge of McClellan Butte above and Alice Lakes below. The trail is rocky and narrow at times and almost always steep except for the short section approaching the peak. The trail curves around the mountain and briefly enters the City of Seattle's Cedar River Watershed, which supplies water for most of the metropolitan Seattle area. Except for this trail and a few trails that run along the border, the Cedar River Watershed is closed to the public to prevent pollution of the water supply. The runner comes to the end of the trail (D) at a bare spot about 100 feet below the summit of the butte. The final climb to the summit is a scramble on slippery rock with steep drops on both sides. Other trail books say the view isn't worth the risk. I didn't go up to find out. Return the way you came. It's very hard to get lost here, but be aware that the trail is on the northeast side of the summit and, therefore, gets dark earlier than the west-side trails. Even a full moon doesn't help light the way through this densely forested approach to the parking area. It was after this run that a small emergency light became part of my standard running equipment.

SIGNIFICANT TRAIL LANDMARKS

A.   Start on Trail 1015.

B.   Go right on the Iron Horse Trail at 0.5 mile.

C.   At 0.9 mile, take Trail 1015 to the left (southwest).

D.   The trail's end just below McClellan Butte. Go back the way you came.

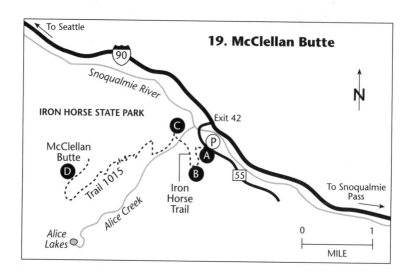

20 PRATT LAKE

Distance	12 miles
Course geometry	Out and back
Running time	4 hours
Elevation gain	3200 feet
Highest altitude	4140 feet
Difficulty	Moderate
Water	40 ounces
Restrooms	Outhouse at trailhead
Permits	Northwest Forest Pass required
Area management	Mount Baker–Snoqualmie National Forest
Maps	USGS Bandera, USGS Snoqualmie Pass, Green Trails #206
Season	July through October

Pratt Lake Trail is the launching point for a number of lakes in the western Alpine Lakes region. Talapus and Olallie Lakes, as well as lakes that lie toward Mount Defiance, are accessible from the Pratt Lake Trail. This is a fun run that climbs through dense old-growth forest. The descent to Pratt Lake has several large areas of scree, but the trail is generally good. The fall-to-spring snowpack results in an inviting summer run with plenty of stream crossings for cooling off or refilling bottles.

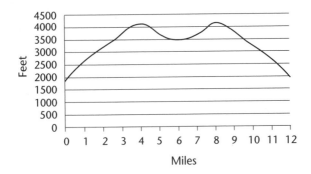

GETTING THERE

From Interstate 90 east of North Bend, take Exit 47 (Asahel Curtis/Denny Creek). Turn left onto the overpass and proceed to a T intersection. Turn left and travel 0.25 mile to the Pratt Lake Trailhead and parking lot.

THE RUN

The Pratt Lake Trail starts at 1830 feet in elevation (A) and climbs steadily to 4140 in 4.3 miles. This is a wide, well-maintained trail through dense forest. The roar of Interstate 90 accompanies you in the first few miles, but then fades. At 1.2 miles there is a junction with the Granite Mountain Trail 1016 (B) and at 3.1 miles there is a junction with a trail leading to Talapus and Olallie Lakes (C). Bypass both of these trails. At 3.5 miles the forest opens to an outstanding view of Olallie Lake and the north face of Mount Rainier. This in itself is worth the trip, and makes a fulfilling turnaround point for a 7-mile run (D).

Soon after the forest opening, you reach a junction with the Mount Defiance Trail 1009 (E), which leads to numerous lakes farther to the west. After another mile descent, including a switchback through a large scree area, you arrive at Pratt Lake (F). From the scree, there is a great view of craggy Kaleetan Peak. Take a short run through the lake basin. The trail comes out on the east side of the lake (G) along another large

Light dusting of snow at 3000 feet

scree area. The lake sits about 30 feet below the rocky trail in a tranquil valley ringed by mountains.

At this point you can retrace your steps for an enjoyable 12-mile trail run or continue on toward Lower Tuscohatchie Lake and connect to the Denny Creek to Kaleetan Lake Trail (Run 18) to add an additional 8 miles. Another option from the Pratt Lake trail is to take the out-and-back Trail 1016 to the Granite Mountain Lookout. The 3.1-mile trail climbs up to 5600 feet in elevation and offers sweeping views of the Cascade Mountains along the Interstate 90 corridor.

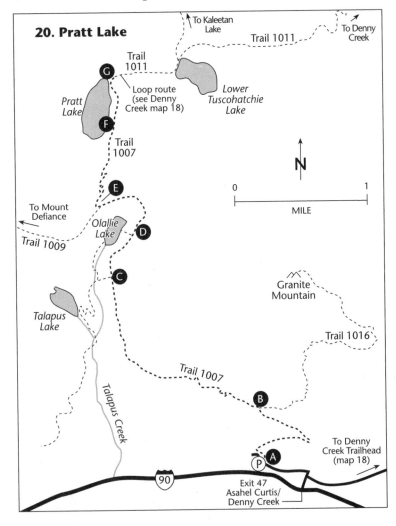

20. Pratt Lake

To Kaleetan Lake

Trail 1011

To Denny Creek

Trail 1011

Trail 1011

Loop route (see Denny Creek map 18)

Pratt Lake

Lower Tuscohatchie Lake

Trail 1007

N

0   1

MILE

To Mount Defiance

Olallie Lake

Trail 1009

Granite Mountain

Trail 1016

Talapus Lake

Talapus Creek

Trail 1007

To Denny Creek Trailhead (map 18)

90

Exit 47 Asahel Curtis/ Denny Creek

SIGNIFICANT TRAIL LANDMARKS

A. Pratt Lake trailhead and parking.
B. Go straight at the junction with the Granite Mountain Trail at 1.2 miles.
C. Go straight at the Talapus and Olallie Lake junction at 3.1 miles.
D. Viewpoint of Olallie Lake and Mount Rainier. Turn around here for 7-mile run, or continue on for Pratt Lake.
E. At 4.5 miles turn right onto Mount Defiance Trail, number 1009.
F. Descend to Pratt Lake.
G. Pratt Lake turnaround or continue for loop route. (See the description for Run 18, Denny Creek to Kaleetan Lake.)

21 KACHESS RIDGE TO THORP MOUNTAIN

Distance	18 miles
Course geometry	Out and back
Running time	6.5 hours
Elevation gain	6120 feet
Highest altitude	5854 feet
Difficulty	Strenuous
Water	60 ounces or bring water treatment supplies
Restrooms	None
Permits	Northwest Forest Pass required
Area management	Wenatchee National Forest
Map	Green Trails #208
Season	June through October

The Kachess Ridge Trail includes an initial rapid ascent, spectacular vistas, and a very narrow section along a precipitous ridge. The view from Thorp Mountain is a 360-degree vista of the surrounding Cascade Mountains, including Mount Rainier and Mount Adams in the distance. There is also a bird's-eye view of Kachess and Little Kachess Lakes. The climbs and the technical running required along the ridge trail make it an excellent outing for the advanced trail runner.

Kachess Ridge, 15 miles east of Snoqualmie Pass, separates 12-mile-long Kachess Lake from Cle Elum Lake. The 5500-foot high ridge rises from the lake at 2200 feet. The fire lookout atop Thorp Mountain still stands, but is unused.

This trail is the finish of the Cascade Crest Classic 100-mile run. Starting in Easton, the race heads west to the Pacific Crest Trail, then north to Snoqualmie Pass, east to Kachess Lake, and then loops back to Easton via the Kachess Ridge Trail and Thorp Mountain. So, for additional challenge, imagine doing this trail after having run 88 miles.

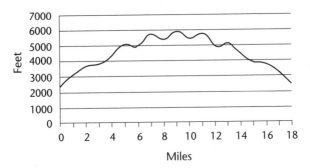

GETTING THERE

From Interstate 90 at Easton, take Exit 70. From the east side of the freeway, turn left on West Sparks Road. After 0.6 mile, turn right on Forest Service Road 4818 for 1 mile. Turn right at a sign for Trails 1315 and 1212. After 0.5 mile look for a small road to the right, along with a parking area. Trail access is 0.1 mile straight ahead.

THE RUN

From the trailhead (A), the Kachess Ridge Trail (Trail 1315) climbs quickly—1000 feet in the first 20 minutes. At mile 1, there is a vista just off the trail looking back on Easton and across to Goat Peak. Continue up Silver Creek Canyon. After the first 2 miles, the trail is not quite as steep. The Beacon Ridge Trail (1315.3), leading to the site of a defunct aero-beacon, branches off at 1.9 miles (B). This beacon was one of several along the Interstate 90 corridor; all now replaced by improved air navigational signals. Continuing on the Kachess Ridge Trail, there are numerous stream crossings as you run through forested areas. As you enter a large meadow at 4.5 miles (C), stop to top off your bottles in the stream (remember to treat all water) running along the edge. There is no natural water for the next 9 miles. The pinnacle rock that forms the left side of the saddle leading to French Cabin Basin looms prominently just beyond the meadow. At 5000 feet in elevation, the saddle looks across to the beginning of the high-country ridge that leads to Thorp Mountain, 3 miles beyond.

French Cabin Basin (D) is a recently logged area, now replanted. Just as you near the ridge on the far side, you reenter old-growth timber. Bypass the French Cabin Creek Trail (E), continuing straight. Once on

Thorp Mountain lookout

the ridge, there will be a number of quick 200-foot ascents and descents. At times, you will be on a rocky and narrow trail overhanging 1000-foot drops. Horses make it safely across this section; take care, and you will too. After several of the short dips along the ridge, Thorp Mountain and the lookout come into view to the north. The ridge trail makes a right turn (to the east) at the signed spur (F) up to Thorp Mountain. The 0.5-mile climb (700 feet in elevation) is well worth the reward of a spectacular 360-degree panorama. There are great views of Mount Rainier as well as the more distant Mount Adams. Head back down from the lookout (G), returning along the ridge to French Cabin Basin. After the 500-foot climb back to the saddle it is a fun downhill run back to the trailhead. Silver Creek and its numerous waterfalls are much easier to enjoy on the return descent.

SIGNIFICANT TRAIL LANDMARKS
A. Trailhead for Kachess Ridge Trail 1315.
B. The Beacon Ridge Trail 1315.3 intersects at 1.9 miles. Continue on Trail 1315.
C. Cross a large meadow and stream at approximately 4.5 miles.
D. Reach the saddle of French Cabin Basin at 5.5 miles.
E. Junction with French Cabin Creek Trail. Go straight.
F. Thorp Mountain Spur Trail leads to the lookout.
G. Lookout and turnaround point.

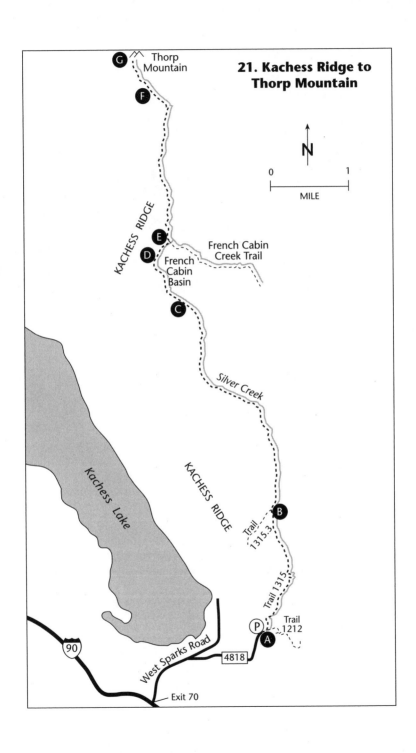

G Thorp
Mountain

F

**21. Kachess Ridge to
Thorp Mountain**

N

0   1
MILE

KACHESS RIDGE

E
French Cabin
Creek Trail

D French
Cabin
Basin

C

Silver Creek

KACHESS RIDGE

B

Trail 1315.3

Kachess Lake

Trail 1315

P
Trail
1212

A

90

West Sparks Road   4818

Exit 70

22 KACHESS LAKE TO SNOQUALMIE PASS

Distance	27 miles
Course geometry	Point to point
Running time	9 hours
Elevation gain	6300 feet
Highest altitude	5730 feet
Difficulty	Strenuous
Water	Need 100 ounces. Bring water treatment supplies. A lot of streams in first 12 miles, none after Park Lakes
Restrooms	Outhouse at trailhead. Bathrooms with water at Box Canyon (Kachess Lake)
Permits	Northwest Forest Pass required
Area management	Alpine Lakes Wilderness and Wenatchee National Forest
Maps	Green Trails #207 and #208
Season	July through October

Local trail runners call this route "the blueberry run." We traditionally make an outing to this trail in August and enjoy wild mountain huckleberries all along the way. The route, combining Mineral Creek Trail and Pacific Crest Trail (PCT), offers a little of everything from steep technical climbs to narrow catwalks and contour-following trails that you can see for miles ahead. The views here are of the "inside wilderness" with alpine lakes, mountain faces, and meadows that you can only see if you're several miles from civilization. The pristine, rugged beauty of this area fills me with awe and appreciation. You will need two cars (one at each end) to do this run.

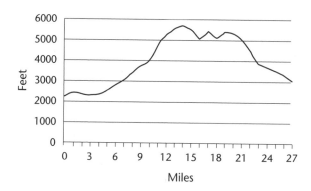

GETTING THERE

For the Pacific Crest trailhead at Snoqualmie Pass, take Interstate 90 east from Seattle to Exit 52, West Summit. Cross under the freeway to the north and look for the signs to the Pacific Crest Trail parking lot. Leave one car here. For the Box Canyon parking area at the start of the run, follow Interstate 90 east of Snoqualmie Pass to Exit 62, Kachess Lake. Turn left and go over the freeway. Follow this road 4 miles to Kachess Lake Campground; enter and turn left to park.

THE RUN

From the Box Canyon parking lot (A) at Kachess Lake Campground, follow Trail 1312, which is across the wood bridge and heads north along the lake. The trail goes up and down, winding away from and back toward the lake. There are some short, steep climbs and gorgeous views of the lake and surrounding mountains. At about 5 miles, you start heading northwest on Mineral Creek Trail (B), an apparent continuation of Trail 1312. The best huckleberries are on the Mineral Creek Trail. There is a sign stating that the trailhead is 5 miles behind you and Park Lakes are 5 miles ahead. The trail follows Mineral Creek to the Park Lakes and goes through sections of dense underbrush in this area. At some points, the trail is barely a tunnel through the brambles. Enjoy the greenness and know that the rest of the trail is wide open. On the way to the lakes there are plenty of streams that may be used for drinking if the water is properly treated first. After the lakes, streams are few and far between. While facing the lakes, look up to a boulder field across the way and see the trail going into it and out of it. Yes, that's the trail you'll be running on, but once you get up there you'll see that it's much easier than it looks. Just past Park Lakes, the Mineral Creek Trail comes to a T intersection with the Pacific Crest Trail (C). Go left and head for the boulder fields. The berries on this segment are nice too.

Cross the boulder fields, passing a sign noting SNOQUALMIE PASS 15 MILES (D), and continue on the Pacific Crest Trail. Way below on your left is Joe Lake. Around the next bend is Alaska Lake, which is a little closer to the trail. From this point there will be more boulder fields and in several places you can look back to see where you were half an hour ago. Finally, a catwalk across scree signals that you are about to start the descent. Like any descent in the Cascade Range, the trail elevation goes up and down, with a net down, for a nice long trip back to about 3000 feet in elevation and the Snoqualmie Pass trailhead for the Pacific Crest Trail (E).

A shorter version of this run is possible with an out-and-back from either end of the trail. From the Snoqualmie Pass side, you reach the ridge in about 5–6 miles with great views of the inner bowls. From

Lynn Yarnall and friends on Mineral Creek Trail

the Little Kachess Lake side, you follow the lakeshore for several miles. The lakeside route has more technical ups and downs, and is quite serene and beautiful with the views all turned upside down on the calm lake surface.

SIGNIFICANT TRAIL LANDMARKS

A. Park second car at Kachess Lake Campground. Cross a bridge and enter Trail 1312.

B. At 4.8 miles, head northwest on Mineral Creek Trail.

C. Reach Park Lakes at 10 miles. Go left at the intersection with the Pacific Coast Trail.

D. Continue past a sign noting the distance to Snoqualmie Pass.

E. Snoqualmie Pass parking for the Pacific Coast Trail.

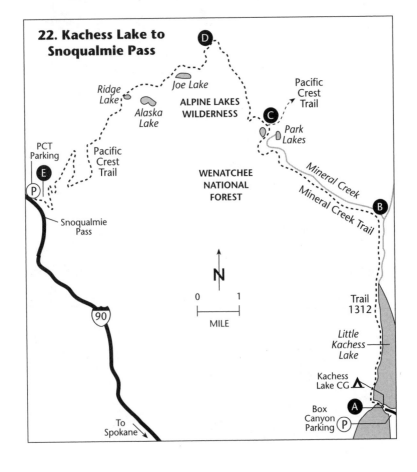

23 SOUTH CLE ELUM RIDGE

Distance	29 miles
Course geometry	Loop
Running time	8 hours
Elevation gain	5600 feet
Highest altitude	5820 feet
Difficulty	Moderate to strenuous
Water	40 ounces
Restrooms	Outhouse at campground
Permits	Northwest Forest Pass required
Area management	Wenatchee National Forest, Cle Elum Ranger District
Maps	Green Trails #240 and #241
Season	June through October

This is a challenging and beautiful course. It is all run on trail, and most of the climbing is in the first half. On the approach to Windy Pass, a panorama of the entire Cle Elum Valley and the Yakima River emerges. In the distance are the Cascade Mountains, particularly Mount Stuart, the largest non-volcanic mountain in the Washington Cascades. Heading east again, the crest of Mount Rainier appears above the closer peaks. The ridge can be cold and windy. Carry a jacket and gloves. Motorbikes keep the trail clear, so expect to see a few. They are very loud and easy to avoid.

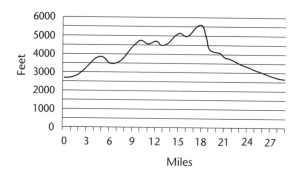

GETTING THERE

From Interstate 90 east of Cle Elum, take Exit 93 (Elk Heights/Taneum Creek). Turn left onto Thorp Prairie Road and follow it for 4 miles. Cross Interstate 90, then turn right on Taneum Creek Road. Continue 8 miles to a primitive camping area on Forest Service Road 3300.

Walking up a steep climb on Cle Elum Ridge

THE RUN

Cross the bridge from the camp area, and go straight to the sign that says TRAIL 1377, TRAIL 1326, 1 MILE. Head up the switchback and to the left. Trail 1326 is clearly signed and is the right fork when the trail splits. If you wish to do the 31-mile route of the Cle Elum Ridge 50K race, go back down the road (east) about 1 mile to the entrance of Trail 1326 (A). This is on Taneum Creek Road at about milepost 7. Trail 1326 connects to Trail 1377 here; however, Trail 1326 is to the right and is more perpendicular to the road.

Trail numbers are only posted in a few places on the whole route. The start is either uphill or level through the woods. At about 3 miles you'll parallel a road for a little while, then cross it as you head west (B). The trail gains 3500 feet, but once on the South Cle Elum Ridge (C) it traverses rolling hills. Once on the ridge, the trail runs parallel to and crosses Forest Service Road 4510 over the course of several miles. A couple of trails intersect with Trail 1326 between miles 10 and 13. Enjoy the view along the approach to Windy Pass (D), but don't turn off Trail 1326. Just short of 14 miles, a sharp turn (E) up a hill takes you through an area that has been recently logged. Descend to a saddle. A 1-mile descent on single track brings you to Windy Pass.

Follow Trail 1326 until just past the pass at 16 miles (F). Turn left here onto Trail 1377, which you stay on almost all the way to the finish. Take the trail down through a deep single track with multiple switch-backs. After you come down from Windy Pass, the trail follows, crosses over, and goes through the north fork of Taneum Creek. There used to be several stream crossings where wet feet were inevitable, but the Forest Service has done a great job of building bridges over many of them. On a hot day, however, splashing through the cold water makes for a very refreshing descent. Just above the parking lot, a single-track trail (G) leaves Trail 1377 to the right and goes directly to the parking lot. If you miss this turn, you will emerge on a road 1 mile past the parking lot.

A shorter version of this run is to run out and back on either Trail 1326 or 1377. Although it is a long run to the ridge from either side, the trail is quite nice following the stream on the 1377 side or running through the forest on the 1326 side.

SIGNIFICANT TRAIL LANDMARKS
A. From the camping area, cross Taneum Creek Road and enter the trail. Take the right fork when the trail splits onto Trail 1326.
B. Cross a road at about 3 miles.
C. Once you reach the ridge, the tough climbs are over.
D. Do not leave Trail 1326 before Windy Pass.
E. The trail takes a sharp left up a logged hill to Windy Pass.
F. Trail 1377 turns left at 16.1 miles. Follow this trail back to the campground area.
G. Turn right onto single-track trail directly above parking lot.

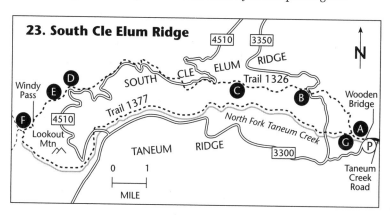

SOUTH CASCADES

Mount Rainier National Park is famous for dense forests, dazzling wild-flower meadows, tremendous snowfields, rugged glaciers, an inland rain forest, and an active volcano! The park's 240 miles of trails are generally accessible from mid- to late June or early July until October, depending on snow depths. The trails here rank among the most beautiful in the Northwest.

Mount Rainier became the fifth national park in 1899. Ninety-seven percent of the area is designated wilderness. Almost 40 percent (91,139 acres) remains covered in old-growth forest. The 204 permanent alpine lakes provide a pristine home to many fish species, including rainbow, cutthroat, and brook trout. Nearly 900 species of flora and 200 species of fauna inhabit the park. The 1-million-year natural history of Mount Rainier is evident in the varying types of lava that layer the mountain and in the glaciers that have cut away the conical shape of the volcano.

Mount Rainier has some of the heaviest snowfall in the country with a record 93.5 feet measured at the Paradise Ranger Station in 1972. The 1999 snowfall came very close to this record. The average snowfall is 52 feet per year. The 14,411-foot mountain is known for creating its own weather. Most of the trails are in the 3000- to 7000-foot elevation zone, where climatic conditions can change rapidly. Be prepared.

24 NORSE PEAK WILDERNESS

Distance	17 miles
Course geometry	Loop
Running time	6.5 hours
Elevation gain	3420 feet
Highest altitude	5920 feet
Difficulty	Strenuous
Water	40 ounces
Restrooms	None
Permits	Northwest Forest Pass required
Area management	Mount Baker–Snoqualmie National Forest
Maps	Green Trails #238 and #239
Season	July through October

The Norse Peak Wilderness loop has some great views of Mount Rainier, Noble Knob, and two alpine lakes, including serene, green-colored Echo Lake, one of the prettiest lakes in the wilderness. Elk frequent the trail, especially in early fall. Hearing an elk bugling during the rutting season is an unforgettable experience.

Portions of this trail are used for the White River 50 Mile Trail Run held yearly in late July. The race starts at Camp Sheppard and runs out to Corral Pass in the first half of the course. The route described here begins at Corral Pass, a popular staging area for backcountry horse expeditions. There are numerous hitching rails between the trailhead and a nearby camping area. Mutton Mountain, which looms just beyond Corral Pass, was named for the large number of sheep that ranged here at one time.

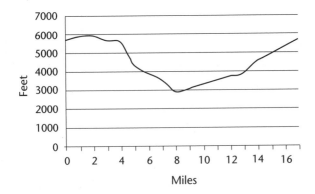

GETTING THERE

From Enumclaw, head east on State Route 410 to milepost 56.2. Turn left on Forest Service Road 7174, a narrow steep road, for the 6-mile climb to Corral Pass. The road is posted as not passable for cars with trailers. Parking is available near the trailhead near the Corral Pass Campground.

THE RUN

For all the distance and trail names and numbers mentioned here, this route follows only three trails: 1184, 1185, and 1176. The Noble Knob trailhead (Trail 1184) exits the Corral Pass Campground on the north side (A). Mount Rainier views are exceptional in the first half mile as the trail starts out level and then slowly rises to 5920 feet in elevation. A large open area skirts Mutton Mountain to your right. At a junction with the Deep Creek Trail (B) (Trail 1196), continue toward Noble Knob on Trail 1184. The trail is narrow through this forested section. The Dalles Ridge Trail (C) goes off to the left; ignore it. After a mile, the trail descends through rocky scree. Noble Knob is directly ahead. Run down a couple switchbacks and stay on Trail 1184 headed east, following the

A late fall snowfall on Corral Pass

signs to Noble Knob. A short side trail out and back to the Knob is definitely worth it during the wildflower season. Devoid of trees, the Knob is usually ablaze with colors.

At an intersection here (D), take Trail 1185 to Lost Lake. As the trail skirts the Knob, you catch a view of the lake below. Go around several rocky protuberances and start a rapid descent into the trees. Between the northwest end of Lost Lake (E) and the smaller Quinn Lake (F), there are several glacial boulder deposits. Numerous streams cross the trail as you continue through the forest on Trail 1185 en route to Trail 1176, also known as the Greenwater Trail (G). Turn right onto 1176 and follow it to a bridge (H). The trail then parallels the Greenwater River for the next 3 miles. The sound of rapids and waterfalls is a constant companion as the trail works its way up to Echo Lake (I). The high rock walls surrounding the lake bounce back echoes, so feel free to let loose with a yip or a yodel. Don't be surprised if a marmot whistles back. There are several campsites along the lake in addition to the stock (horse) camps.

At the southwest end of the lake (J), continue on Trail 1176 to Corral Pass. The ascent to the pass starts out very gradual and is mostly runnable except for a few miles of switchbacks. Take a sharp right to stay on Trail 1176 at an intersection with Trail 1188 (K). The trail ends back at the Corral Pass Campground (L). One-quarter mile to the right, you will find the hitching rails and your starting point.

SIGNIFICANT TRAIL LANDMARKS

A. Parking and trailhead.
B. Deep Creek Trail (1196) enters from the left; continue toward Noble Knob.
C. Dalles Ridge Trail (1173) enters from the left; continue toward Noble Knob.
D. The Noble Knob (1184), Noble Knob Summit (1184.1), and Lost Lake (1185) Trails converge. Take the right fork toward Lost Lake.
E. Lost Lake lies to the right of the trail at 5.8 miles.
F. Quinn Lake is less than 1 mile beyond Lost Lake.
G. Intersection with the Greenwater Trail (1176). Make a sharp right (south) onto Trail 1176.
H. Trail 1186 approaches from the left at 11.4 miles. Stay to the right on Trail 1176.
I. Pass Echo Lake on the left.
J. Intersection with Arch Rock Trail (1187). Go straight and stay on Trail 1176.

K. At 16.2 miles, Trail 1188 intersects Trail 1176. Stay on Trail 1176
    by making a sharp right toward Corral Pass Campground.

L. Corral Pass Campground, you're done!

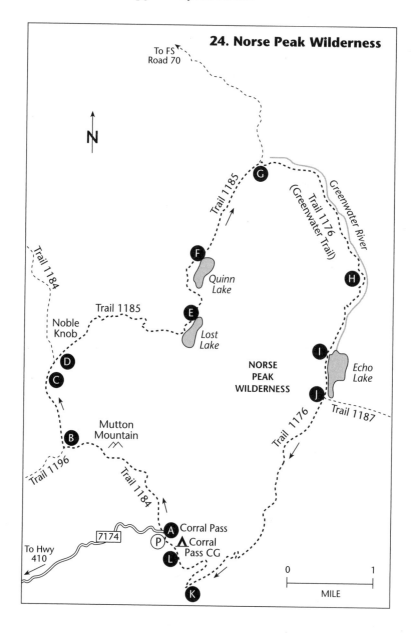

24. Norse Peak Wilderness

25 MOWICH LAKE

Distance	17 miles
Course geometry	Loop
Running time	6 hours
Elevation gain	4500 feet
Highest altitude	6300 feet
Difficulty	Strenuous
Water	40 ounces
Restrooms	Outhouse at trailhead
Permits	National Park permit required (available at park boundary)
Area management	Mount Rainier National Park
Maps	Mount Rainier National Park Map, Green Trails #269
Season	July through October

This trail is scenic, well maintained, and almost entirely runnable. You pass waterfalls, wildflower meadows, majestic glaciers, old-growth forests, and towering rock formations, all on a 17-mile loop on Mount Rainier's north face. Streams along the way provide plentiful water that can be treated for drinking.

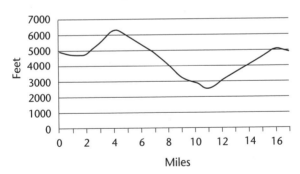

GETTING THERE

From Puyallup, drive 13 miles east on State Route 410 to Buckley. Turn right (south) on State Route 165 and left at the Y intersection of State Routes 162 and 165. Proceed through historic Wilkeson and past Carbonado. Just beyond the Carbon River Gorge Bridge, bear right onto Mowich Lake Road. Follow the road about 17 miles to its end; the trailhead is on the south side of the Mowich Lake Campground. Mowich Lake Road closes with the first snow of the season (October or November)

Nearing Isput Pass

and typically does not reopen until July. The last 10 miles of road is gravel and can be dusty and full of washboard ruts late in the season.

THE RUN

From the trailhead (A) on the south side of Mowich Lake Campground, follow the Spray Park Trail to Eagles Roost Camp and Spray Falls just beyond (B). To get a good look at the falls, walk about a tenth of a mile on a spur trail, then slightly out on the rocks. The falls tower above you and are quite spectacular. From the falls continue toward Spray Park (C) on a steep, upward switchback section of trail.

As you emerge through the tree line, several lovely sights await you. On a day in September the wildflowers were blooming, two marmots were posed on rocks, and the fabulous, glacier-covered peak of Rainier greeted us around every bend. On foggy days, after leaving the meadows watch carefully for rock cairns that mark the route on the fields of rocks and snow. After reaching the high point at 6300 feet in elevation (D), the view to the north includes far-off Mount Baker, Glacier Peak, and a sweeping look at the Cascade Range. To begin the descent to Cataract Camp (E), we glissaded for a quarter mile in a large snowfield.

Continue down through old-growth forest to the Carbon River Camp (F). The total elevation drop is 3000 feet in 4 miles. We made a brief diversion onto a short trail leading to the Carbon River Suspension Bridge. The bridge is quite a thrill and provides a head-on view of the Carbon Glacier and its namesake river. You may have to wait your turn since the bridge is close to vehicle access and very popular. Come back across the bridge to where you were, then go right on the Wonderland Trail (Run 26), the 93-mile trail circumnavigating Mount Rainier. The Wonderland Trail follows the Carbon River while dropping to 2400 feet, the lowest elevation of the loop. You pass Ipsut Falls (G) and continue on a very runnable surface with lovely surroundings. The trail passes through an inland rain forest with moss covering all the rocks and hanging from the trees. Cross several streams with wood bridges and start the ascent to Ipsut Pass (H). Yes, you are climbing to those huge jutting rocks that seem to be miles above you. The rock formations with black stripes are very interesting. We also found salmon berries on the climb that scored a 10 on a scale of 1 to 10. Just as you wonder where they put the next switchback (you're about to run into the rock wall), you'll see a little treed slot between the rocks to the left. This is Ipsut Pass, 5100 feet in elevation and only about 200 feet higher than Mowich Lake. As you approach the lake from above, you can see much of the bottom through the crystal clear water. The campground and trailhead are less than a mile away.

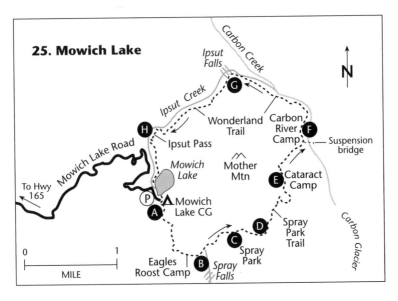

SIGNIFICANT TRAIL LANDMARKS

A. Spray Park Trail starts on the south side of Mowich Lake Campground.

B. Spray Falls, a spur trail to view the falls, is at 2.3 miles.

C. Spray Park is at 4.4 miles. Continue on Spray Park Trail.

D. High point on route, 6300 feet.

E. Cataract Camp. Continue to Carbon River.

F. Carbon River Camp and the Carbon River Suspension Bridge. Detour to view the glacier from the bridge, then head north (right) on the Wonderland Trail.

G. Ipsut Falls at 11.2 miles. Follow to Wonderland Trail to the left.

H. Ipsut Pass is a slot between the rocks.

26 WONDERLAND TRAIL

Distance	17.5 miles
Course geometry	Out and back
Running time	6 hours
Elevation gain	5270 feet
Highest altitude	6760 feet
Difficulty	Moderate to strenuous
Water	40 ounces
Restrooms	None at trailhead, outhouses at Summer Land and Indian Bar Camps
Permits	National Park permit required (available at park boundary)
Area management	Mount Rainier National Park
Maps	Mount Rainier National Park Map, Green Trails #270
Season	July through October

This trail is well maintained, almost entirely runnable, and incredibly beautiful. You pass through old-growth forests, by waterfalls, and over meadows of wildflowers. Mountain goat herds often can be seen on distant hillsides. The Fryingpan, Emmons, and Ohanapecosh Glaciers are constantly in view, and the nearby rock formations provide a constant geological study. For the last several years, this high portion of the Wonderland Trail has seldom been free of snow during the July through October period, but the trail is marked so you won't lose it. There is plentiful stream water along the way that can be treated for drinking.

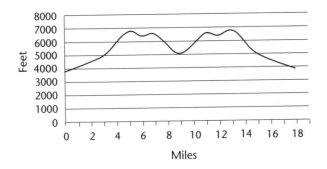

GETTING THERE

From Enumclaw, drive 43 miles east on State Route 410 to the Mount Rainier National Park White River Entrance. Proceed 3 miles to the limited parking area near the Fryingpan Creek Bridge. The trailhead is across the road. There are additional parking areas 1 mile in either direction.

THE RUN

From the trailhead at 3900 feet in elevation (A), follow the Wonderland Trail southwest along Fryingpan Creek. The trail starts out very wide, passing through dense old-growth forest. Go up several large switchbacks that offer some excellent views of the creek and an occasional waterfall. In about 3 miles, you reach the upper valley leading to Summer Land (B). Fryingpan Glacier and Little Tahoma Peak (11,138 feet in elevation) appear in front of you. Off to the right is Goat Island Mountain. The Emmons Glacier and Mount Rainier summit loom just ahead. The views are breathtaking from Summer Land Camp. People who bring cameras frequently remark that they wish they'd brought more film. From the hill behind the hiking shelter at Summer Land, you can see steps across the valley leading up through the high terrain across from you. That's your path, the Wonderland Trail, proceeding to Indian Bar (E) 4.5 miles away.

Continue on the Wonderland Trail up to Panhandle Gap (C) at 6760 feet in elevation, the high point on this route. The climb up to the gap is like traveling through a moonscape. The trail is across rock with no vegetation. At times, the andesite rocks are green on one side of the trail and brown on the other side. The majestic Fryingpan, Emmons, and Ohanapecosh Glaciers are in constant view. As you near Panhandle Gap, you may have to traverse slippery snow patches. As late as October I have encountered snow left from the previous winter.

Emmons Glacier and Little Tahoma Peak

Once clear of the Gap, look back to your left across the valley (D). There are often mountain goats near the top of the Cowlitz Chimneys. Look for the white spots. Once again, there are waterfalls and more glacial views around every turn in the trail. The Wonderland Trail stays near the 6500-foot level for about a mile farther. Mount Adams and the southern Cascade Range form the panorama ahead. As you begin the 2-mile, 1500-foot descent to Indian Bar (E) you can make out the three-sided stone shelter in the meadow far below. Along the trail in this area you may see signs of elk or, if you're lucky, the entire herd. The little stone shelter that you saw from the top of the hill finally comes into clear view as you enter Indian Bar. Cross the creek at Wauhaukaupauken Falls, and you're there. Take a snack break, soak in the scenery, refill the water bottles, and head back. Because of the stunning vistas that seem to change with the time of day and the direction of travel, the trip back from Indian Bar is just as interesting as the trip in. The snow can be a little trickier on the downhill. Be careful.

For a shorter, but also nice run, turn back at Summer Land Camp for a round trip of 8 miles and plenty of photo opportunities.

SIGNIFICANT TRAIL LANDMARKS

A. Follow the Wonderland Trail southwest along Fryingpan Creek.

B. Summer Land Camp. Turn back here for an 8-mile round trip or continue on the Wonderland Trail.

C. Panhandle Gap is the high point on the trail. Take care going over snow patches.

D. View of the Cowlitz Chimneys.

E. Indian Bar Camp. Turn around and go back the way you came.

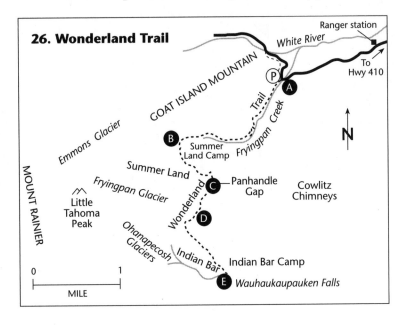

OLYMPIA

The Capitol State Forest lies within the Black Hills just 5 miles south of Olympia. The forest encompasses 90,125 acres and has more than 400 miles of well-maintained, runnable trails. The views are outstanding. Mountain bikes, hikers, and trail runners are allowed on all trails year-round. Horses and off-road vehicles (ORVs) are allowed on the trails from April through October only. To avoid conflicts, the north trails are open to motorized bikes and ORVs while the south trails are open to horses. With an ORV park adjoining the forest, the trails can be busy at times. Logging activity is common. Capitol Forest is an example of the leading edge of forest management technology.

The Black Hills formed about 12 million years ago when the sea floor was pushed against the western edge of North America. The sea floor folded, compressed, and pushed up above sea level. You can find shellfish fossils in forest's sedimentary rock. The northern and eastern edges of the forest feature hundreds of shaped mounds formed by glaciers depositing gravel in the area. The two high points in the forest are Capitol Peak (2659 feet) and Larch Mountain (2660 feet).

27 CAPITOL PEAK

Distance	9.4 miles
Course geometry	Out and back
Running time	2.5 hours
Elevation gain	1550 feet
Highest altitude	2659 feet
Difficulty	Easy to moderate
Water	40 ounces
Restrooms	Outhouse at trailhead
Permits	None required
Area management	Department of Natural Resources (DNR)
Map	DNR Capitol State Forest
Season	Year-round

On a clear day you can see from the ocean to the mountains, including Mount Olympus, Mount Baker, Mount Rainier, and Mount Adams. The sweeping views are a highlight of this run. This trail starts at Wedekind Picnic Area and follows the ridge to Capitol Peak, offering outstanding views at several points along the way.

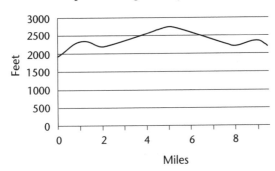

GETTING THERE

From Interstate 5 at Olympia, take Exit 104 and follow U.S. Highway 101 west for 2 miles. Take the West Olympia, Black Lake exit and head south on Black Lake Boulevard. Go 4 miles to a T intersection. Take a left on Delphi Road, then a right on Waddell Creek Road, and go past the Delphi Entrance to a Y junction. Take the right fork 1.4 miles to a split. Go left on C-Line Road (also signed C-2000 in places). Stay on C-Line Road 7 miles to a junction on the ridge crest (2150 feet in elevation). Turn left on Forest Service Road B-2000, a continuation of C-Line, for

1.5 miles to Wedekind Picnic Area on the left and parking on the right near the trailhead.

THE RUN

Go up Porter Creek Road across from the picnic area and turn right onto Trail 30 in a few hundred feet. Follow this for 0.3 mile until you come to a set of signs. One of them is the Greenline 6 Trail. Turn right onto Greenline 6 (A) and follow this trail almost to the peak. (We turned left and had a very nice 4-mile diversion.) The trail is well maintained, well marked, and runnable. It follows the gently rolling ridge through grass, salal, and huckleberry brush. Basalt rocks poke through the soil. Wildflowers bloom abundantly through spring and summer. On the right are Sherman and Chehalis Valleys. Porter Valley and all the fingerlets of blue water and green peninsulas of south Puget Sound are on the left. Larch Mountain and the many-towered Capitol Peak loom ahead.

Vista from Capitol Peak

You cross the C-Line Road twice on the route. At the first crossing (B), pick up the trail just across the road. There is a sign. The second time, you must go a little to the right from the junction (C), then go left on a smaller road. In a few hundred feet, you will see the clearly marked Greenline 6 Trail on the left. Head up to the crest at 2450 feet of elevation then drop to the saddle at 2150 feet. The final half-mile is on a spur road (D). Capitol Peak and all its communications towers are at 2659 feet of elevation (E). Head back the way you came. The gradually rolling trail down is quick and pleasant.

Use caution when driving out. The logging roads are not well marked. When leaving, follow the C-Line back to the Waddell Creek Road; exit the forest at the Delphi entrance. It is 8 miles back to the highway.

SIGNIFICANT TRAIL LANDMARKS

A. Go up Porter Creek Road and turn right onto Trail 20 for 0.3 mile, then go right onto the Greenline 6 Trail.

B. Cross C-Line Road at 1 mile. Pick up trail on opposite side of road.

C. Recross C-Line Road. Go slightly right on the road, then left on a smaller road for a few hundred feet to a trail marker for Greenline 6 Trail.

D. A road takes you the final half-mile.

E. Capitol Peak is 4.7 miles in.

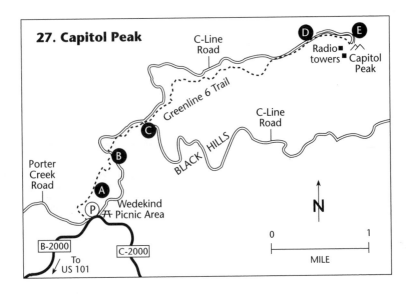

28 ROCK CANDY MOUNTAIN

Distance	18.5 miles
Course geometry	Loop
Running time	5.5 hours
Elevation gain	3700 feet
Highest altitude	2360 feet
Difficulty	Easy to moderate
Water	40 ounces
Restrooms	Outhouse at trailhead
Permits	None required
Area management	Department of Natural Resources (DNR)
Map	DNR Capitol State Forest
Season	Year-round

Rock Candy Mountain, the northernmost of the three highest peaks in the Black Hills, has the best views of saltwater inlets at the southern end of Puget Sound. A network of well-maintained trails allows long runs through forests of cedar, hemlock, and fir.

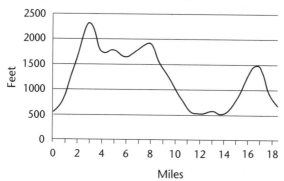

GETTING THERE

From Interstate 5 at Olympia, take Exit 104 west onto U.S. Highway 101 and continue 10.7 miles to just past milepost 17 and turn left onto State Route 8. There is a low sign pointing south to Rock Candy Mountain and north to Summit Lake. Head south and enter the off-road vehicle trailhead area.

THE RUN

From the parking lot, head toward Rock Candy Mountain on the road. Cross under the powerlines and enter the trail on your left (A).

The sign says ROCK CANDY MTN. WEST. Head up this wide, well-maintained dirt bike trail until you come to a Y intersection (B). This is the intersection with the Rock Candy Mountain East Trail, which will be your return route. The west trail to the right goes up a little ways, crosses a road, then stays more level until you cross another dirt road. The trail intersects the North Rim Trail here (C); go left. After traveling uphill for about 0.5 mile, you come to another junction with the North Rim Trail, which winds around on its way to the north boundary of Capitol State Forest. A sign says ROCK CANDY SUMMIT 1.3 MILES. Pick up Road B-8500 and make the climb to the summit.

North from Rock Candy Mountain

The road wraps around the mountain, giving you 360 degrees of panorama through the vegetation. At the top of Rock Candy Mountain there are no trees to block your view. You can see from Puget Sound on the west to the Cascades on the east. Between them are the easily recognizable cooling towers for the mothballed Satsop Nuclear Plant on one side and the dome of the capitol building in Olympia on the other. Follow the road for a fast-paced downhill return to the trail. If you want to limit your run to 9 miles, continue straight at the intersection of the North Rim, Rock Candy West, and Summit Trails (D), then follow the instructions from (G) to return to your car.

For the 18.5-mile route, go right at the intersection (D). Follow the contour of the mountain for a few miles. The trail parallels Road C-8000. When you get almost to the major logging road, C-4000, do not cross the road, but make a sharp left onto Mount Molly Trail (E). Follow Mount Molly Trail as it continues to contour, then parallels Road C-8200 and drops several hundred feet in elevation toward Waddell Creek. The trail curves back to the right; then there is a sharp left. Soon after, pick up the North Rim Trail (F) and parallel Road C-8000 and Waddell Creek. Continue almost straight on the North Rim Trail for about 4 miles, then start the switchbacks up. Cross Road B-8500, and within 0.5 mile you come to the junction of Rock Candy East and the point where the 9-mile route joins the 20-mile route (G). Turn left if you did the short route, turn right if you're on the longer route, and follow Rock Candy East steeply down, under the powerlines and back to your car.

SIGNIFICANT TRAIL LANDMARKS

A. Trailhead and parking. Enter trail on the left from road.

B. Junction of Rock Candy Trail East and West. Go right on Rock Candy West.

C. Join Road B-8500 to summit at 2 miles. Go right.

D. Go left on the North Rim Trail for a 9-mile route, then pick up the instructions again at (G) for the shorter run; go right for the 18.5-mile route.

E. Junction at 5.5 miles with Road C-4000 and Mount Molly Trail. Go left from the road onto the trail.

F. Turn left onto North Rim Trail, paralleling Road C-8000 and Waddell Creek.

G. Junction of 9-mile and 18.5-mile routes. Go left on Rock Candy East from shorter route, go right from longer route, to return to your car.

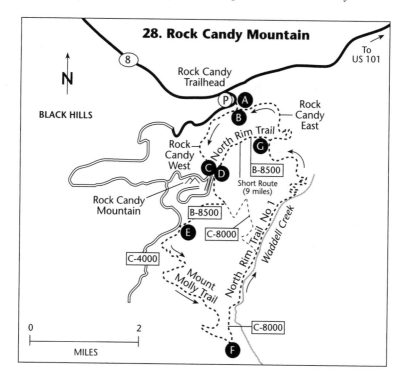

29 LARCH MOUNTAIN

Distance	7 miles
Course geometry	Out and back
Running time	2 hours
Elevation gain	1200 feet
Highest altitude	2659 feet
Difficulty	Easy
Water	40 ounces
Restrooms	Outhouse 5 miles from the start
Permits	None required
Area management	Department of Natural Resources (DNR)
Map	DNR Capitol State Forest
Season	Year-round

This route takes a logging road to the summit. There is rarely traffic on the road. You can forget about the worries of motor bike encounters on a narrow trail, yet still enjoy all the views of the trail routes.

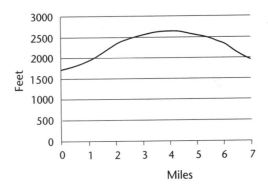

GETTING THERE

From Interstate 5 at Olympia, take Exit 104 west onto U.S. Highway 101. Go 10.7 miles just past milepost 17 and turn left onto State Route 8. There is a low sign pointing south to Rock Candy Mountain and north to Summit Lake. Head south and enter the off-road vehicle trailhead area on the B-Line Road. Park here for a 17-mile run that includes the road referenced for the 7-mile run. For the 7-mile run, continue on the road to a powerline junction after the road narrows about 1.5 miles from the ORV parking. Take the left fork uphill. Another fork appears; again go left. This road is marked as ROCK CANDY MTN. ROAD. Three miles up this road, a jeep road appears on the left. Find a wide spot on the road here to park.

THE RUN

From the Rock Candy Mountain Road parking area (A), take the right-fork road, Road C-4000 (was Rock Candy Mtn. Road). Go straight. The beginning portion heads down before it goes back up again. You will pass a road on your left signed as MT. MOLLY LOOP (B). Continue up the hill. At a big intersection of four muddy roads (C), go straight. Road C-4000 continues almost 3 miles from the jeep road start or 8 miles from the ORV parking at the big lot at the base of the mountain). At the end of the road you'll reach a fork with a huge yellow gate (D). Run up the gated road on switchbacks to the summit of Larch Mountain. Note that the mountain is earning its keep with communications towers by the summit (E). On a clear day you can see the chiseled face of Mount Olympus and the Pacific Ocean.

If you prefer, a woodsy trail also climbs the north side of Larch Mountain—see the DNR map for this trail. Be aware that it is a single-track trail and shared with mountain bikes and motor bikes.

Steve Wells and the approach to Larch Mountain's summit

SIGNIFICANT TRAIL LANDMARKS

A. Fork to Rock Candy Mountain and Larch Mountain. Park where you can.
B. Run 1.3 miles to sign for Mt. Molly loop. Continue on road.
C. Four-way intersection. Go straight.
D. Fork with yellow gate. Take a sharp right onto Larch Mountain Summit Road.
E. Larch Mountain summit. Return the way you came.

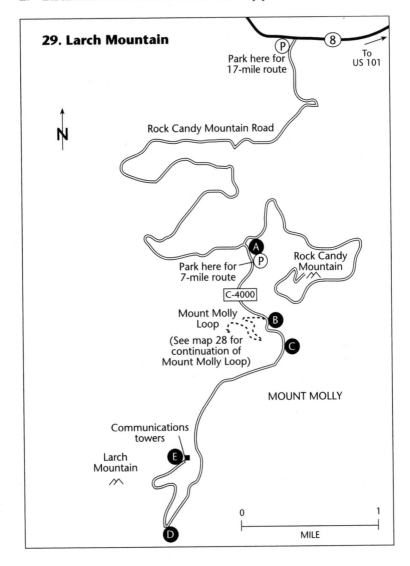

29. Larch Mountain

Park here for 17-mile route

8

To US 101

N

Rock Candy Mountain Road

A

P

Park here for 7-mile route

Rock Candy Mountain

C-4000

Mount Molly Loop

(See map 28 for continuation of Mount Molly Loop)

B

C

MOUNT MOLLY

Communications towers

E

Larch Mountain

D

0   1

MILE

EASTERN WASHINGTON

Eastern Washington appears to be a different country than Western Washington. From the high desert of the Ellensburg/Yakima area to the dry plains of inland Washington, a great diversity of trails emerge. Another kind of beauty exists in these lands. There are miles and miles of undeveloped land. The scents of sage and pine can be strong under the warmth of the sun. And there's little underbrush to hack through. However, water is not around every corner as it is in Western Washington. Sunburn, rattlesnakes, and dehydration need to be considered seriously here.

Although there are many beautiful places to run along the Columbia River, as well as in the Okanogan region, I have limited my coverage to areas that are easily accessible from the Interstate 90 corridor. The Mountaineers Books publishes a more extensive trail guide to the region called *100 Hikes in the Inland Northwest*.

30 MANASTASH RIDGE

Distance	10 miles
Course geometry	Out and back
Running time	2.5 hours
Elevation gain	2140 or 3100 feet
Highest altitude	3922 feet
Difficulty	Easy to moderate
Water	40 ounces
Restrooms	None
Permits	None required
Area management	Washington Department of Fish and Wildlife
Map	USGS Manastash Creek
Season	Year-round, with snow in winter

This run is easily accessible from Ellensburg and Interstate 90. Depending on the route you choose for the ascent/descent, you can have a steep quad killer or a more runnable meandering trail. Whichever path you choose, you're going to get some hill work.

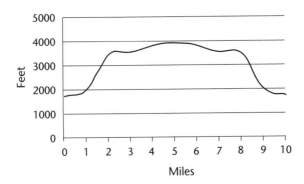

GETTING THERE

From Interstate 90, take Exit 106, Ellensburg. Follow Main Street for about 1.5 miles as it becomes Canyon Road and turn left at the McDonald's restaurant. Follow Dammon Road, going west, and cross the Yakima River near Irene Rhinehart Park. The road curves left (south). Next to Damman School, turn right onto Manastash Road and go 3 to 4 miles until you reach Cove Road. Take a left on Cove Road. Drive about 0.2 mile and park in the lot just off the road on the right.

THE RUN

From the parking area, go straight on the road (A) as it becomes a smaller jeep road, then curves off to the right to head toward the base of the ridge on single-track trail. It is a 2-mile run to the top of the ridge on any one of several trails. One option is to go south up the hill—look for a plank over an irrigation ditch, follow the jeep trail for 0.3 mile, and then look for a steep trail on the right going up the ridge (B). Another option is to follow the jeep trail farther along the irrigation ditch, then turn left up a trail (C) that goes along a creek at the low point between the hills. This route is bordered by spring flowers and has some nice shade on hot days. The steepest trail to the top lies between these other two and is easy to see from below (D). It goes right along the outer edge

David Lygre on trail

of the hillside corner. Whichever route you choose, follow it to the top, where there's a logbook to sign in (E). There is also a memorial to Allan Westburg, a well-loved teacher who used to run on this trail. Turn around here for a shorter, 4-mile run.

Cross the ridge from the logbook and look to your right (west) where you will see a white dome in the distance that is the University of Washington Manastash Ridge Observatory (F). Follow the jeep road here 3 miles to the observatory and turn around there. There are expansive views of Ellensburg and the Yakima Valley. This area also overlooks the L.T. Murray Recreation Area to the northwest and south (see Run 31). Once back at the logbook, you can take any of the trails down. They will either follow the jeep road or the irrigation ditch near the bottom. Both head back to where you parked.

SIGNIFICANT TRAIL LANDMARKS

A. From the parking lot go straight on the road as it becomes a smaller jeep road and curves right.
B. First option for ascending ridge is an easy-to-follow jeep trail.
C. Second option is to follow the irrigation ditch and go left on the trail along the stream.
D. Third option is to follow the irrigation ditch and turn left onto the trail that goes up the face of the ridge. This is the steepest approach.
E. Top of the ridge and logbook. Turn around here for a 4-mile run.
F. The University of Washington Observatory. Return the way you came.

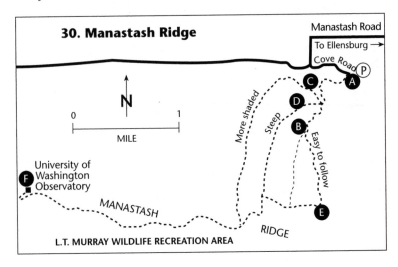

31 YAKIMA CANYON RIM

Distance	16 miles
Course geometry	Out and back
Running time	4 hours
Elevation gain	4200 feet
Highest altitude	3208 feet
Difficulty	Moderate to strenuous
Water	80 ounces
Restrooms	Outhouse at trailhead
Permits	None required
Area management	Washington Department of Fish and Wildlife
Maps	USGS Badger Pocket 15 minute and Pomona 7.5 minute, Washington Department of Game Yakima Canyon Rim Trail Map
Season	Year-round, with snow in winter

The Yakima Rim Trail is part of the L.T. Murray Wildlife Recreation Area above Selah. It is a beautiful example of the dry, sage-scented high desert lands of central Washington. The 100,000-acre preserve harbors many types of wildlife. The long list starts with elk, mule deer, and white-tailed deer, and continues with coyotes, rabbits, buzzards, grouse, and pheasants. I was told to look out for rattlesnakes, but I never saw or heard any. Magpies and hawks dominated my wildlife viewing when I visited this trail on a July day. There are many wildflowers in the spring.

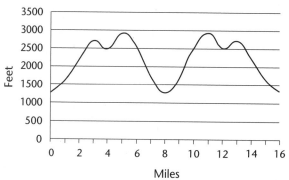

GETTING THERE

From Interstate 82/U.S. Highway 97 just north of Yakima, take Exit 26 (Firing Center). Proceed west on Canyon Road for 0.7 mile to Harrison Road, and turn left. After 2 miles turn right onto North Wenas Road. After 2.8 miles it will curve sharply to the left; continue straight onto a

Roza Dam and the Yakima River below the first summit

dirt road (Gibson Road). Within a quarter of a mile turn right (east) onto Buffalo Road. Go 2.75 miles past farms and through grasslands to a gated parking area with an outhouse.

THE RUN

From the parking lot (A), follow the road a short distance north to the trailhead (B). The trail is easy to follow and is marked with horse trail signs or at least the signposts without the sign. This dusty landscape with its rolling hills and weather-beaten signposts has the look of the old West. Heading up to the ridge from the trailhead, you'll keep thinking you see the summit, only to go over a ridge and see the next "summit" (it's the old "where's the summit?" game).

The long climb to the first summit (C) (elevation 3000 feet) takes about one hour. Once there, you will see an overlook with a few rock and wood structures. The trail turns down and to the left briefly before continuing east along the ridge. Roza Dam stands out far below on the Yakima River. Each time you come around the southeast side of a peak, the winding Yakima River and the railroad come into view below, assuring you that you're on the right trail. To the west you will see Mount Rainier and Mount Adams, a sight you don't see from many points in Western Washington. Follow the trail north and go through twin springs and a pleasant oasis (D). Don't let the noisy magpies drive you away. Horse troughs collect the small amount of water put out by the springs. It doesn't look good to drink, though some hiking books claim it is. It's definitely great for dumping over yourself on a hot day.

From the spring, climb back up to the ridge and to the second summit (E) (elevation 3000 feet). Take the long, steep trail (F) down to Roza Creek, almost to the road (G). Although the trail continues for miles beyond this point, it is hard to follow and the grass is filled with burrs. If you want to continue, wear gaiters. My socks and shoes looked like porcupines after a few miles through the grass. There is a stream in the grassy area, so if you need water and have the supplies to treat the water, get it here. The trail continues up to Umtanum Ridge (H), where it becomes an old wagon road. Elk herds gather in this grassy area in the fall.

When you've put in all the miles you want for the day, turn around and follow the same route back to your car. There is also a north trailhead near Ellensburg, but the route described here stops 8 miles out at Roza Creek. Beyond Roza Creek, a campground toward the Yakima River is a source for emergency water.

SIGNIFICANT TRAIL LANDMARKS

A. Parking area. Cross road to trailhead.
B. Trail goes north from road.
C. Two miles to the first summit. Trail turns downhill to the left then heads toward the next summit.
D. Twin springs with a water trough marks halfway point.
E. Second summit is at 6 miles. Follow steep trail downhill almost to the road.
F. Roza Creek is the turnaround point.
G. Continue across meadow for a longer run.
H. Umtanum Ridge.

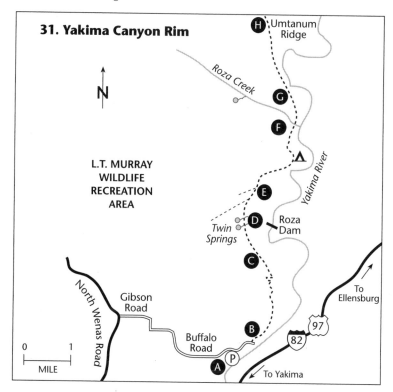

32 MOUNT SPOKANE

Distance	10 miles
Course geometry	Out and back
Running time	2.5 hours
Elevation gain	2230 feet
Highest altitude	5282 feet
Difficulty	Moderate
Water	40 ounces
Restrooms	Outhouse at trailhead
Permits	None required
Area management	Mount Spokane State Park
Maps	USGS Mount Spokane and Mount Kit Carson, updated trail map available at park headquarters
Season	June through October

Forest, meadow, burping brooks, and mountain vistas are all offered on this 10-mile, out-and-back run. The trail goes rather steeply up almost all the way to Mount Kit Carson, then is fairly flat between Mount Kit Carson and Day Mountain. Cooler and moister than the valley below, this trail can be a refreshing run on a hot summer day.

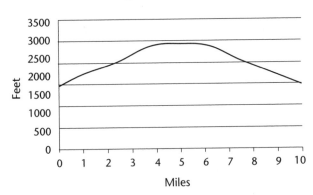

GETTING THERE
From Interstate 90 in Spokane, take Exit 281. Follow U.S. Highway 2 until you reach Mount Spokane Park Drive, which is State Route 206 (easily visible signs). Travel 15 miles on Mount Spokane Park Drive. The trailhead for Trail 115 is on the left just before the entrance to Mount Spokane State Park.

Vista from Day Mountain

THE RUN

Enter Trail 115 on the right side of the clearing that is on the left side of Mount Spokane Park Drive (A). If you're lucky, a deer will be standing there to greet you. Trail 115 soon splits from Trail 155 (B). They join again within a mile as Trail 115, so take either one. The trail is wide, well maintained, and well marked all the way. On your right, Burping Brook gurgles in the distance. The trail joins a fire road (C) and passes Smith Gap Picnic Area on the right. At Smith Gap, go to the left on the road and then pick up the trail on the other side. The elusive deer would stand and look at me until I got them into view with my camera, then they'd bound away. From Smith Gap, the trail climbs steeply to Grouse Meadow (D). Continue on Trail 115 around the summit of Mount Kit Carson (elevation 5282 feet). Enjoy the abundant wildlife, including birds, rabbits, and deer. They must know there's no hunting in this park.

Once near the summit, you have a choice (E) between Trail 115 and Trail 170. Trail 170 goes to the summit, while Trail 115 skirts the summit. Both trails join at the northeast end (F). However, if you take Trail 170 from (E), turn left after 0.5 mile onto Trail 130, which takes you to Day Mountain. If you choose to follow Trail 115 past Mount Kit Carson, you will need to go left on Trail 170 at its north end for a short ways to get to Trail 130 (G), where you'll turn right.

The route to Day Mountain first goes down steeply and becomes more moist and meadowlike as you approach the summit. Here the deer seem to take a route perpendicular to the trail, while the rabbits, as

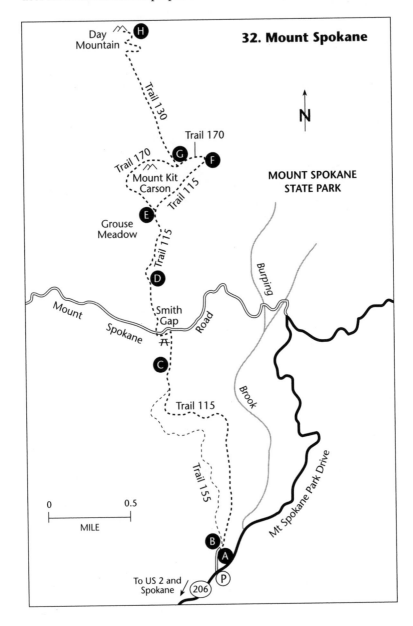

usual, are hopping around independently on their own agenda. The wildflowers, which are spectacular in the spring and early summer, are still blooming well into August. There is a rock outcropping and cairn at the peak of Day Mountain (elevation 5057 feet) (H), where you can look out to the north and east at Spokane, little towns beyond, and the Cascade Range in the distance.

SIGNIFICANT TRAIL LANDMARKS

A. Pick up Trail 115 from clearing on left side of Mount Spokane Road.
B. Trails 115 and 155 split, rejoining in a short distance.
C. Trail becomes fire lane, then passes the Smith Gap Picnic Area and crosses Mt. Spokane Road.
D. Trail climbs steeply to Grouse Meadow.
E. Trail 115 splits with Trail 170. Take either one.
F. Trails 115 and 170 rejoin. Go left on 170 for short distance to reach Trail 130 from this side of Mount Kit Carson.
G. Trail 130 to Day Mountain. Go north onto trail.
H. Day Mountain summit and overlook. Turn around and return the way you came.

33 DISHMAN HILLS

Distance	5 miles
Course geometry	Loop
Running time	1.5 hours
Elevation gain	600 feet
Highest altitude	2350 feet
Difficulty	Easy
Water	20 ounces
Restrooms	Restrooms and water at trailhead
Permits	None required
Area management	Department of Natural Resources (DNR)
Maps	DNR Dishman Hills, USGS Spokane NE
Season	March through October

This gently rolling trail passes outcroppings of 1.5-million-year-old layered rock, ponds, grasslands, shrublands, and forest. The trails are well maintained and fairly well marked. The route provides a pleasant, hilly workout. There is ample parking with restroom facilities and water at the Camp Caro entrance.

The Dishman Hills Natural Resources Conservation Area is characteristic of the Spokane Valley before it was settled. In addition to the rugged landscape and the abundance of wildflowers, the area is visited by coyotes, weasels, squirrels, chipmunks, marmots, porcupines, white-tailed deer, hawks, ruffed grouse, pheasants, and more than 50 species of butterflies. I had the pleasure of seeing many of these animals in just two trips through this area.

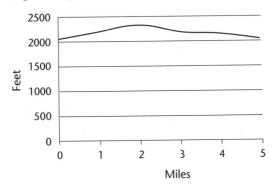

GETTING THERE

From Interstate 90 in Spokane, take Exit 285 (East Sprague). Go 1.75 miles, then turn right on Sargent Road. Drive about half a mile on Sargent Road to the public parking area at Camp Caro.

THE RUN

From the Camp Caro parking lot, walk through the archway in the building to find the trail entrance in front of you (A). Head south on the Goldback Springs Trail past Caro Cliff to the springs at 0.7 mile (B). Shortly after the springs, turn right onto Tower Mountain Trail (C). Continue on Tower Mountain Trail for 0.6 mile, then turn right (west) onto Eagle Peak Loop Trail (D). Detour right on the short spur to Eagle Peak and back (E). Mount Spokane rises to the north, while the vista to the east overlooks the industrial area of Dishman Hills and is topped by the mountains of Idaho. Continue on Eagle Peak Loop Trail until it intersects with Ridge Top Trail (F). Turn right (north) on Ridge Top Trail and follow it through the pine forest and shrubland. Rejoin Tower Mountain Trail (G) by curving to the left at the intersection, then turn left onto Pond Loop Trail (H). Follow this to another left on Birch Hollow Trail (I). On Birch Hollow Trail stay to the right whenever there is a choice. This will put you on Edgecliff Trail (J). Edgecliff Trail comes to a T intersection with Pond Short Trail (K). Turn right to see the nearby ponds,

Steven Pierce and dog friend

which may be dry indentations by the end of summer. Turn around here and follow Pond Short Trail across its intersection with Pond Loop Trail (L) back to the parking lot.

SIGNIFICANT TRAIL LANDMARKS

A. The entrance to the Goldback Springs Trail is through the archway in the building. Head south.

B. Goldback Springs at 0.7 mile.

C. Turn right onto Tower Mountain Trail.

D. Turn right (west) onto Eagle Peak Loop.

E. A short spur to the right takes you up and back to Eagle Peak.

F. Intersection of Eagle Peak Loop and Ridge Top Trails. Turn right (north) onto Ridge Top Trail.

G. Rejoin Tower Mountain Trail by curving to the left at the intersection.

H. Turn left onto Pond Loop Trail.

I. Turn left (west) onto Birch Hollow Trail. Stay right as you run.

J. Take a right onto Edgecliff Trail.

K. Edgecliff Trail ends at Pond Short Trail. Go right to see the ponds; go left to return to the start.

L. Intersection of Pond Short and Pond Loop Trails. Go left to return to Camp Caro parking lot.

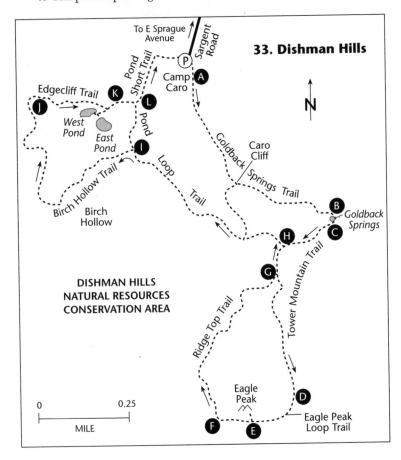

34 ROCKS OF SHARON

Distance	8 miles
Course geometry	Loop
Running time	2 hours
Elevation gain	1840 feet
Highest altitude	3600 feet
Difficulty	Moderate
Water	40 ounces
Restrooms	No
Permits	None required
Area management	Bureau of Land Management
Map	USGS Spokane SE
Season	March through October

All the ultrarunners I've met from the Spokane area use this trail frequently for training. It has some great steep climbs, incredible rugged beauty with large rock outcroppings, and "top-of-the-world" views encompassing Steptoe Butte, Mount Spokane, and beyond. These trails are not marked, so bring your topographical map and compass if you're not running with someone who knows the trails. The wildlife listed in Dishman Hills (Run 33) also can be seen on this route, which is just south of the Dishman Hills Natural Resources Conservation Area.

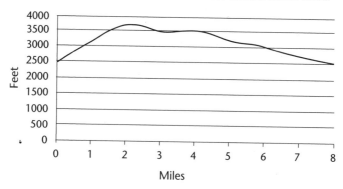

GETTING THERE

From Interstate 90 east of Spokane, take the Argonne exit and head southeast on Dishman–Mica Road. Turn right onto 44th Street. Follow 44th for about a mile, then go left on Farr Road, then right on Holman Road. The trailhead is at the end of Holman Road. There is room on the side of the road for a few cars and a trash can at the trailhead.

The Rocks of Sharon

THE RUN

We started out by going right (north) at the trailhead (A), saving the best visual treat (Big Rock or Rocks of Sharon) for last before the descent. After about 100 feet, head back south on the trail (B) toward the radio tower (C). Cross two jeep trails and continue uphill and southwest to the radio tower. Approaching the tower, take the jeep road (D). It crosses in front of the radio facilities building. Go directly south along the ridge toward the second set of radio towers (E). Passing on the left (east) side of this radio tower, follow the ridge and take the trail that curves off to the left (east) from the ridge. The trail is fairly flat for a while, then goes up, then down, and up again to some rocky protuberances. You can see Steptoe Butte in the distance from the edge of the rocks. If you have a camera, don't take too many photos at the first rock outcropping, because it gets better. It can be hot and dry along this area. Go downhill again, then back up to what the map calls Big Rock (F) but what some of the local ultrarunners refer to as the Rocks of Sharon. This, in my opinion, is one of the most picturesque places in the entire Spokane region. In addition to the fabulous vistas, the light and shadows from the towering rocks make for a transfixing scene. Leaving the panorama, go downhill to the northeast from the rocks, up another hill, then down the trail. When there are places to turn on this trail, go left. Follow the contour of the hills (G) from 3100 feet in elevation to 2900 feet in elevation over 2 miles. On trail intersections, take the route that goes downhill. You will cross three streams that may be little more than moist dirt, depending on the time of year. After about 3 miles the trail joins a jeep road (H) that is an extension of Holman Road where you parked.

SIGNIFICANT TRAIL LANDMARKS

A. Go north from trailhead.

B. Make a right onto southbound trail toward radio tower.

C. The first radio tower is at 2.2 miles.

D. Follow a jeep road to the left of the radio facilities building.

E. Second set of radio towers. Go straight past towers and take the trail curving downhill to the left (east).

F. The Big Rock or Rocks of Sharon are at 4 miles. Go northeast from the rock formation.

G. Begin following contours from 3100 feet in elevation to 2900 feet in elevation over next few miles. Go down when there is a choice of trails.

H. Jeep road leads back to Holman Road.

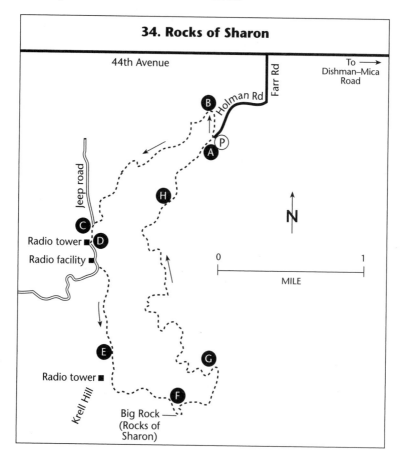

34. Rocks of Sharon

35 LIBERTY LAKE PARK

Distance	7 miles
Course geometry	Loop
Running time	2.25 hours
Elevation gain	1340 feet
Highest altitude	3140 feet
Difficulty	Moderate
Water	30 ounces
Restrooms	Restrooms at trailhead
Permits	$2 parking fee during summer season
Area management	Liberty Lake Parks Department
Map	Trail map available at entrance booth
Season	March through October

This gem of a trail is mostly shaded and cool. It follows Liberty Creek, crosses the creek here and there on footbridges, then crosses and follows the waterfall up the hill to the ridge. After the midpoint, enjoy a fast and continuous downhill dash to the valley. The trail in the area approaching and passing the waterfall is rugged and steep. The rest of the trail is well maintained and well marked.

Liberty Lake County Park is 1 mile wide and 5 miles long. It has been an active recreation site since the first settlers arrived in 1871. The historical information on the back of the hiking map is quite interesting. It talks about the area going from roadhouse to a respectable summer resort to a ranch. Finally in 1966, it was purchased by Spokane County with matching funds from federal and state agencies to become the Liberty Lake Natural Area.

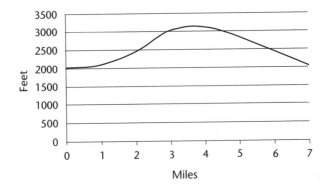

Warning near a cedar grove on Liberty Creek

GETTING THERE

From Interstate 90 east of Spokane, take the Liberty Lake exit onto Liberty Lake Road. Immediately take a left (east) onto Appleway. Drive 0.75 mile and turn right (south) on Molter Street. Drive another mile or so and turn left (east) on Valleyway. Follow Valleyway about 2.3 miles. It may change names, but there are signs to Liberty Lake County Park. The park is open April 15 through October 15, and an attendant can give you a map with this trail on it. In the off-season, park by the water tower above the entrance and go around the entrance gate. During the summer months you can park in many parking areas inside the gate along the road to the trailhead. The trailhead is at the back of the campground to the right. June through Labor Day, there is a $2 fee for anyone over 6 years of age.

THE RUN

The trail starts and finishes on flat ground just past a large trail map sign (A). You pass a picnic table, a horse corral, and two sitting benches then move onto a woodsy trail. At Split Creek Crossing (B), cross the bridge and continue up either the left or right side of the creek. At Skull Creek Camp Crossing (C), continue on the trail to the right side of the creek. The trail meanders back and forth across the creek. At Cedar Forest Camp (D), cross a wooden bridge and follow the steep switchbacks to the west until the trail levels again. In less than a mile from the last crossing, you'll come to the waterfall with 100-foot cascades. The trail is rather rugged in this area due to erosion. Cross a wooden bridge with railings and continue up the switchbacks toward the right, to the top of the falls, then continue on the left side of the creek, passing two additional smaller falls upstream. At 3.2 miles, another wooden bridge (E) takes you to the right side of the creek. Cross the bike trail, going uphill, until you come to an outhouse, then turn right down a gentle slope to Camp Hughes Cabin (E). From the cabin, you start a gentle 3-mile descent on the bike path. As used here, "gentle" means you can go as fast as you want because the trail has few if any obstacles and is not too steep. At about 6 miles, you come to a gate and a sign that says EDITH HANSON RIDING TRAIL (F). Continue straight, cross the bridge, run across the open meadow (can be very hot in the summer), run over a culvert bridge, and you're back to the original trail near the horse corral. It's 0.5 mile back to the trailhead. If it's a hot day, a dip in the lake adds the perfect finishing touch to this delightful run.

SIGNIFICANT TRAIL LANDMARKS

A. Trailhead is at back of campground to the right, about 0.5 mile from the entrance.

B. Split Creek Crossing. Cross bridge and continue up left or right side of creek.

C. Skull Creek Camp Crossing is at 1.4 miles. Go up the right side of the creek.

D. Cedar Forest Camp and another bridge. Head west up switchbacks.

E. At 3.2 miles, turn right at the outhouse and down the slope to Camp Hughes Cabin.

F. In about 3 more miles there is a sign that reads EDITH HANSON RIDING TRAIL. Continue straight. Cross bridge, cross open meadow, and rejoin original trail near the horse corral.

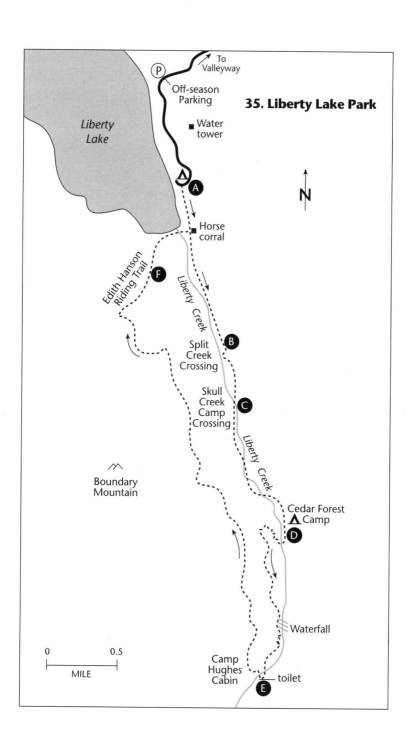

To
Valleyway

P

Off-season
Parking

35. Liberty Lake Park

■ Water
tower

*Liberty
Lake*

N

Ⓐ

△

→

■ Horse
corral

Edith Hanson
Riding Trail

Ⓕ

Liberty Creek

→

Ⓑ

Split
Creek
Crossing

Skull
Creek
Camp
Crossing

Ⓒ

Liberty Creek

⌃⌃
Boundary
Mountain

Cedar Forest
△ Camp

Ⓓ

↑

→

↓

Waterfall

Camp
Hughes
Cabin

⌐ toilet

Ⓔ

0   0.5
├────┼────┤
   MILE

URBAN TRAILS

I grew up in Burien and West Seattle. In Burien I would play in the landscaped bank on the edge of our apartment complex pretending I was in the woods. Later in West Seattle I remember trying to become lost in Lincoln Park, spending lots of time in the vacant lots (thing of the past), feeling hidden in the woods. With parents who favored other urban areas for vacation destinations, I became adept at finding "nature" in cities.

The fact that I can go from Bothell to the Columbia River by using the Tolt Pipeline, Snoqualmie Valley, and Iron Horse Trails is incredible. In the densely populated Bellevue area, I can run from Lake Washington to Lake Sammamish with only a few blocks here and there on road. Large woodsy areas in the cities have been recovered from the private sector for parklands, offering a refreshing and convenient respite from the concrete and metal landscape of city life. They're there for you; use them!

36 ST. EDWARDS STATE PARK

Distance	8 miles
Course geometry	Loop
Running time	1.5 hours
Elevation gain	1200 feet
Highest altitude	390 feet
Difficulty	Moderate
Water	20 ounces, refillable at restroom
Restrooms	At picnic area near the parking lot and at the bottom of Seminary Trail
Permits	None required
Area management	Washington State Parks and Recreation Commission
Maps	Maps posted at trailhead
Season	Year-round

St. Edwards State Park offers more than 7 miles of meandering forest and waterfront trail, which can be combined to create a scenic and challenging workout. The trails traverse up and down the high bank of the waterfront, meeting fairly level connector trails at the shore and along the bluff. The park land has been logged, was privately owned for a time as a country home, and was then sold to the Archdiocese of Seattle, which ran St. Edwards and St. Thomas Seminary (now Bastyr University). Finally the land was sold to the state for a park.

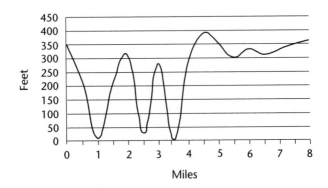

GETTING THERE

From Interstate 405, take Exit 20A, NE 116th Street. Go left (west) off the exit ramp. Follow 116th, continuing through the intersection at

Trail through the ravine at St. Edwards Park

98th NE, to Juanita Drive NE. Follow Juanita Drive north 3.5 miles, enter the park, and follow the road to the right.

From State Route 522 (Bothell Highway) turn south onto 68th Avenue NE, which is also Juanita Drive NE. Go up the hill 1.8 miles to the entrance to St. Edwards Park and Bastyr University. Follow the road to the right for the north parking lot.

THE RUN

From the north parking lot behind the gym you will find a trail map and the sign for the North Trail (A). Follow the North Trail a little to the north, then around the west side of a steep ravine. Descend 0.6 mile to Lake Washington (B), then follow the trail south along the tree-lined waterfront until you come to Seminary Trail (C). There are primitive toilets near the trail junction. Go left on Seminary Trail, which climbs 330 feet while meandering 0.6 mile through lush green trees and nettles near the path. The well-maintained trail connects with the Perimeter Trail (D) bordering the parking lot and following the ridge at the top of the bluff. Go right on Perimeter, headed south past the Grotto (E) to the steep Grotto Trail. In a mere 0.5 mile you'll find yourself back at the toilets, Seminary Trail, and the shoreline (C). Head south again along the shore a short distance to South Canyon Trail. Run up South Canyon Trail until it intersects with the Orchard Loop Trail (F). Since there are five trails traversing the bluff, one trail will have to be done twice to get you back to your car. The trip around Orchard Loop and back down South Canyon Trail works well for this. Pick up the South Ridge Trail just north of the entrance to South Canyon at the shore. The South Ridge Trail climbs to the high point of 390 feet in elevation in its mile. Once back at the top, turn left to follow the Water Tower Trail (G), then make a right turn to pick up the Plateau Trail and continue past Bastyr University across the road you drove in on. When you reach the Juanita Trail you can make a nice cool-down loop on the Juanita, Arrowhead, and Volunteer Trails (H) (approximately 1 mile total). Follow the perimeter trail back to the parking lot and north trailhead (A).

SIGNIFICANT TRAIL LANDMARKS

A. Trailhead for North Trail is at the north parking lot behind the gym.
B. North Trail meets Lake Washington. Go left (south) along the shore.
C. Seminary Trail and toilets. Go left (east) up the hill.
D. Perimeter Trail go right (south) along the parking lot.
E. Follow Grotto Trail, which returns you to the Seminary Trail. Head south to the South Canyon Trail.
F. South Canyon intersects with Orchard Loop Trail. Go left (north) and around the loop, then back down South Canyon Trail.
G. Go left onto Water Tower Trail, then right (north) onto Plateau Trail.
H. Choose Juanita, Arrowhead, or Volunteer Trail to descend back to the trailhead.

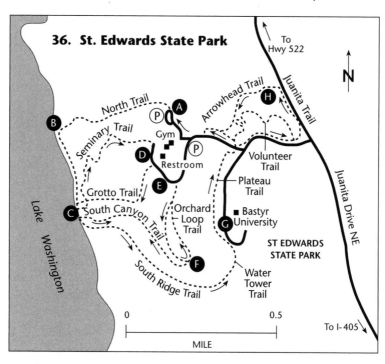

36. St. Edwards State Park

To Hwy 522

N

Arrowhead Trail

Juanita Trail

North Trail

Seminary Trail

Gym

Restroom

Volunteer Trail

Plateau Trail

Grotto Trail

South Canyon Trail

Orchard Loop Trail

Bastyr University

Juanita Drive NE

Lake Washington

South Ridge Trail

Water Tower Trail

ST EDWARDS STATE PARK

0   0.5

To I-405

MILE

37 TOLT PIPELINE

Distance	16 miles
Course geometry	Out and back
Running time	4 to 6 hours
Elevation gain	3250 feet
Highest altitude	1000 feet
Difficulty	Easy to moderate
Water	40 ounces
Restrooms	At Blyth Park and on the Sammamish River Trail; both have drinking water
Permits	None required
Area management	King County Parks
Maps	Various trail books
Season	Year-round

The Tolt Pipeline is a 100-foot-wide, 12-mile-long trail for foot, horse, and bicycle use. The Seattle Water Department built the pipeline in

1963 to bring water from the Tolt River Reservoir to the city. It acquired
a strip of land 100 feet wide and, with the help of King County Parks,
established the 12-mile route as a park. It has great steep hills, dirt and
gravel surfaces, and runs from Bothell to the Snoqualmie River Valley.
The trail is well maintained and there is enough traffic that it's safe to
run alone. This is a great place to develop your hill running muscles
without having to worry about the tricky footing on mountain trails.
The main drawback is that it crosses several major roads, including
Interstate 405, if you take it all the way from Blyth Park.

The section described here leads from the Sammamish River to the
Snoqualmie Valley in about 8 miles, all of it runnable. This section is
mile 4 through 20 on the elevation profile and gives you 16 miles out and
back. However, the profile also includes the section west of the Sammamish River. I'm thrilled by the fact that you can get from the heart of
Seattle to the Columbia River on a network of trails and this is one
of the links.

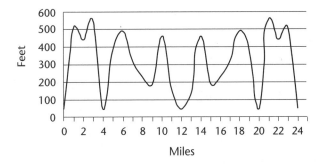

GETTING THERE

There are usually two to four parking spots at each trail and street
intersection, but the simplest place to park is along the Sammamish
River Trail on 145th Street in Woodinville (refer to map 37 East). From
Interstate 405 take the 124th Street exit and head east across the valley
to the Woodinville–Redmond Road (State Route 202). Turn left and
proceed north to a left turn onto 145th Street. Then take a right just
before the river into the parking lot for the soccer and baseball fields.
The Redhook Ale Brewery and Chateau St. Michelle Winery are directly
west of the parking lot across the river.

THE RUN

From the Sammamish River Trail parking lot (A), head north past
the bathrooms about a tenth of a mile. You'll see a swath of clear-cut on

the hills on both sides of you. Turn right onto the Tolt River Pipeline heading east. After a short distance on flat trail, you'll cross the Woodinville–Redmond Road (B). Be careful; this is a heavily traveled road, and the pedestrian crossing sign is easy to miss. Once across the road, head up a series of hills past new houses and pastures. The section of the trail crossing 155th Street used to go down on the road, but a very nice pedestrian bridge is now in place on that section. Once across this bridge, the trail continues up and alongside more large homes and farms.

Several miles of the Tolt Pipeline Trail

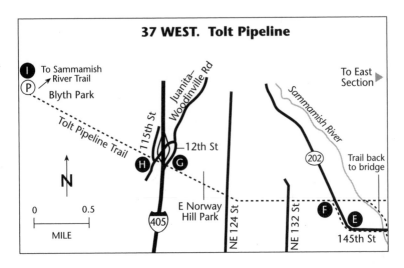

The next major crossing is Avondale Road (C), which is approximately 4 miles from the Sammamish River Trail. There is additional parking here. Once across Avondale, the trail stays fairly level for a while, then goes up once more through another area of new homes. The trail seems to come to an end as you near the Snoqualmie River (D). This is the turnaround point. However, if you really want a long run, go down the driveway to the right, turn north onto West Snoqualmie Valley Road for 0.5 mile, then turn east onto NE 124th Street. Go another mile across the very narrow bridge over the Snoqualmie River and join the Snoqualmie Valley Trail (Run 43).

Back at the starting point (A) on Map 37 West, if you wish to continue west to Blyth Park in Bothell, head south from the 145th Street parking lot to the footbridge that goes over the Sammamish River. Wind through the Redhook Brewery trails (E) or follow State Route 202 (now on the west side of the river) north until you see that clear-cut swath (F) again and head up. It is less than 4 miles from the Sammamish River to Blyth Park. When you reach Juanita–Woodinville Road, turn right and cross Interstate 405 on the 160th Street overpass (G). The pedestrian lights don't get you everywhere you want to go, and you have to go through a new housing development on the east side of Interstate 405 to pick up the trail again. This is not a trail runner's idea of fun. When you get to 115th Street from Juanita Road, go right until you see the familiar clear-cut strip again (H). From there, the route is straightforward until it comes out under a powerline above Blyth Park. You can try to

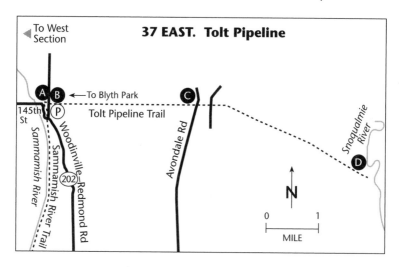

find an unmarked trail through the woods or go down the steep powerline path until you see a trail through the woods, then follow it down. You will eventually come out in Blyth Park. If you've left the car back at 145th Street and don't want to go back the way you just came, take the Sammamish River Connector Trail (I) out of Blyth Park on the north side of the entrance and head southeast. Go along that trail for about 5.5 flat miles. You'll have the bathrooms on your left, Redhook Brewery on your right, and your car in the parking lot.

SIGNIFICANT TRAIL LANDMARKS

A. From the parking lot, head north past the restrooms.
B. Cross Woodinville–Redmond Road.
C. Cross Avondale Road.
D. Trail ends at 8 miles near the Snoqualmie River. Turnaround point.
E. Cross bridge over river to Redhook Brewery. The Tolt Pipeline Trail is not continuous here.
F. Follow State Route 202 north until you see clear-cut on the left.
G. To cross Interstate 405, take Juanita Road (right) north to the 160th Street overpass.
H. Continue on Juanita Road to 115th Street, turn right (north), and again look for clear-cut and pipeline trail on left.
I. Trail ends above Blyth Park. Return the way you came or follow the Sammamish River Connector Trail southeast from the north side of the park entrance.

38 REDMOND WATERSHED AND PUGET POWERLINE TRAILS

Distance	15 miles
Course geometry	Out and back with loop
Running time	4 hours
Elevation gain	1060 feet
Highest altitude	560 feet
Difficulty	Moderate
Water	40 ounces, water at Farrel McWhirter Park
Restrooms	Farrel McWhirter Park, outhouse at Redmond Watershed main parking lot
Permits	None required
Area management	City of Redmond Parks and Recreation Department
Maps	Watershed map available at main parking lot. Maps posted at every intersection on the trail. Puget Power Trail and connector from King County Thomas Guide
Season	Year-round

The Redmond Watershed Trail in itself is a great run with gently rolling hills, well-maintained trail, directions at each intersection, and wildlife. I have seen beaver, deer, and countless birds in this forest oasis in the middle of bustling Redmond. For a longer run with real hills, I have added the Puget Power Trail.

GETTING THERE

The Puget Power Trail starts approximately 2.3 miles north of Marymoor Park from the Sammamish River Trail. From State Route 520 east

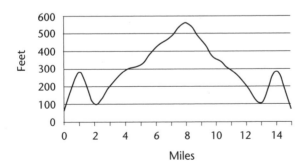

of Interstate 405, take the West Lake Sammamish Parkway exit. Go south on West Lake Sammamish Parkway. There's a traffic light at the entrance to Marymoor Park. There are also parking lots along the Sammamish River Trail at the 1-mile point (behind Shari's Restaurant), at the 2.5-mile point (near Redmond Court House), and at the 116th Street soccer fields (approximately 3.2 miles north of Marymoor Park).

THE RUN

From the entrance to the Puget Power Trail (A) at approximately the 2.3-mile point on the Sammamish River Trail, run up the switchbacks, and following the powerline, cross Avondale Road. There is one place where the trail jogs to the left along a road (B), but it is marked. The Puget Power Trail currently ends at the north end of Farrel McWhirter Park (C), though there is talk of continuing the trail to the Redmond Watershed. There are bathrooms and water in the park.

From the Puget Power Trail, pick up the road (D) to the Redmond Watershed at the northeast corner of Farrel McWhirter Park. Follow the road to the left until you reach 116th Street (E). Go uphill (east) on

Approaching the Redmond Watershed from McWhirter Park

116th until you reach 209th Avenue (F). Turn left on 209th and continue running until you see a sign announcing the Redmond Watershed (G). An entrance here puts you on Old Pond Trail. Go straight. For the 5.5-mile outer loop of the Redmond Watershed, take a left onto Trillium Trail (H) off of Old Pond Trail, then head east (right) on Pipeline Trail (I) about 0.25 mile to Collin Creek Trail (J). Turn left. Go 0.5 mile on Collin Creek Trail to Siler's Mill Trail (K). Turn right and continue 1.35 miles, curving left onto Pipeline Regional Trail for 0.75 mile to a right onto Trillium Trail (L). The main parking lot (M) and toilet are on the left near this trail. This is a good starting point if you don't want to do the hills of the Puget Power Trail. To continue, follow Trillium Trail back to Old Pond, then onto 209th, and retrace your steps.

SIGNIFICANT TRAIL LANDMARKS

A. From the 116th Street parking lot, go left 1.1 miles to the entrance of the Puget Power Trail.
B. Trail jogs left along a road. Follow signs to trail.
C. Trail ends on north side of Farrel McWhirter Park.
D. From northeast corner of Farrel McWhirter Park, go left on road to Redmond Watershed.
E. Turn right onto 116th Street.
F. Go left on 209th Avenue.
G. Entrance to Redmond Watershed and Old Pond Trail. Go straight.
H. Turn left onto Trillium Trail.

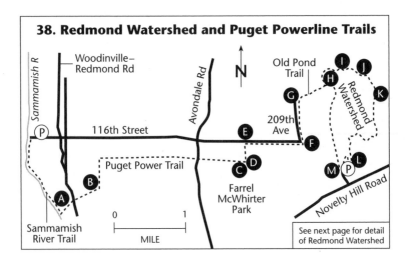

38. Redmond Watershed and Puget Powerline Trails

Sammamish R

Woodinville–
Redmond Rd

Avondale Rd

N

Old Pond
Trail

Redmond Watershed

P

116th Street

209th
Ave

Puget Power Trail

Farrel
McWhirter
Park

Novelty Hill Road

0   1

Sammamish
River Trail

MILE

See next page for detail
of Redmond Watershed

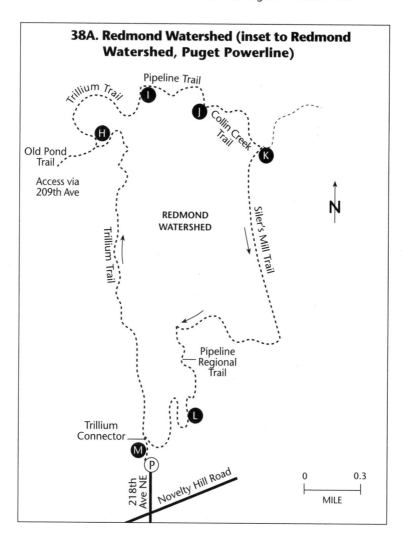

38A. Redmond Watershed (inset to Redmond Watershed, Puget Powerline)

I.   Go right onto Pipeline Regional Trail.
J.   Go left onto Collin Creek Trail.
K.   Turn right onto Siler's Mill Trail for 1.35 miles. Trail curves left onto Pipeline Trail for 0.75 mile.
L.   Turn right onto Trillium Trail. Follow to a left onto Old Pond Trail and return the way you came.
M.   Parking lot for Redmond Watershed. Park here for shorter run.

39 DISCOVERY PARK

Distance	2.8 to 8 miles
Course geometry	Loop
Running time	30 minutes to 2 hours
Elevation gain	500 feet or less elevation gain
Highest altitude	300 feet
Difficulty	Easy
Water	Not necessary, but one bottle to refill at restrooms is nice
Restrooms	Toilets and drinking fountains
Permits	None required
Area management	Seattle Department of Parks and Recreation
Map	Map available at visitor center
Season	Year-round

Many seasoned trail runners go to Discovery Park for its convenience and beauty. With 534 acres, more than 7 miles of trails, forest, saltwater beaches, a lighthouse, and spectacular views of Puget Sound, the Olympic Mountains, and Mount Rainier, it is an ideal urban getaway.

Many of the Puget Sound Indian tribes, including the Shilshoh, Duwamish, Suquamish, Tulalip, White, and Green River peoples, used the Discovery Park area in times past. Evidence indicates it was used as a village site, fishing station, and for shellfish and plant gathering and hunting beginning more than 2700 years ago. While digging for the sewage treatment plant in 1992, archeologists found evidence of fire pits for drying clams and fish and bone tools. Petrified wood from the Columbia River and obsidian artifacts from Oregon indicated that trading had occurred between tribes.

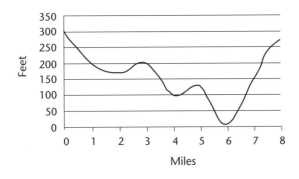

The City of Seattle donated the land to the government to build Fort Lawton. However, Fort Lawton was declared surplus in 1972, and most of the land came back to the city to make a park. Military buildings and housing are still identifiable. Discovery Park is considered to be one of the best places in Seattle for viewing birds, with 253 types identified. It is the nesting area for 50 bird species, including the bald eagle. Information on the plants and birds of the area is available at the visitor center.

The lighthouse at Discovery Park

GETTING THERE

From downtown Seattle, follow Elliot Avenue north along the waterfront. It becomes 15th Avenue. Continue to the West Dravus Street exit and turn left at the stop sign. Turn right onto 20th Avenue West, which becomes Gilman Avenue West, then West Government Way, and follow the signs to the park entrance. The visitor center, where you can park and pick up a map, is here. There is also a north parking lot near Commodore Way and a south parking lot off West Emerson Street. Maps showing access to the Loop Trail are posted at both parking lots. The run described here begins from the south parking lot, which is about 0.75 mile southwest of the visitor center.

THE RUN

This run can be shorter or longer depending on how many circuits you make on the basic Loop Trail and whether you add excursions to the West Point Lighthouse or other side trails. To begin, head west out of the south parking lot on the Loop Trail (A). You see your first view of the Olympics when the trail turns right after passing the restrooms (B). Run along the top of the bluff here. It's fortunate there are few obstacles on the trail, because it's hard not to look out at the sweeping view of Puget Sound and Mount Olympus. On your first trip through the park, go past the sign for the South Beach Trail (C) and continue past the military housing on Dakota Street. The Loop Trail continues through the woods and is marked the entire way, although many of the signs have been vandalized. This trail passes the visitor center (D) and takes you back to the south parking lot. This loop is about 2.8 miles.

On the second trip along the Loop Trail, you may wish to turn left onto the South Beach Trail (E). This will take you down some stairs, past a beautiful view of Mount Rainier, and then to a sidewalk (F) leading down to the beach 300 feet below the bluff. From here you will see another trail (G) that runs to the lighthouse and past a drinking fountain. From the lighthouse (H), head north on the North Beach Trail, which passes the sewage treatment plant. Near the end of the beach there is a sign in the woods for the North Bluff Trail (I). Take that trail back inland to the Loop Trail, which leads back to your car. This second loop is about 5 miles.

The park's north parking lot (J) provides access to the Wolf Tree Nature Trail, which goes through forest on a wood chip trail and leads to the Daybreak Star Indian Cultural Center. In the past you could go from the North Bluff Trail to the cultural center on the North Bluff Road, but parts of the road slid down the cliff in the wet winter of 1996 and at this writing the road has not been repaired or rerouted.

SIGNIFICANT TRAIL LANDMARKS

A. Head west out of the parking lot on the Loop Trail.
B. Pass the bathrooms and head right along the bluff.
C. Pass South Beach trailhead and stay on Loop Trail.
D. Continue straight on the trail past the visitor center.
E. Trail to South Beach, which leads to the water.
F. A sidewalk here leads to the beach.
G. Follow trail to lighthouse.
H. Lighthouse. Take the North Beach Trail north past sewage treatment plant.
I. North Bluff Trail starts in the woods. Follow it back to the Loop Trail, which leads back to parking lot.
J. The Wolf Tree Nature Trail from north parking lot to cultural center. Add to run if desired.

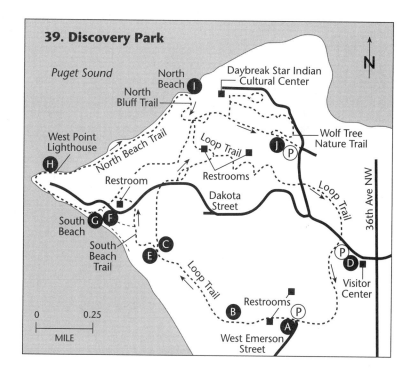

40 BRIDLE TRAILS STATE PARK

Distance	4.8 miles
Course geometry	Loop
Running time	1 hour
Elevation gain	260 feet
Highest altitude	460 feet
Difficulty	Easy
Water	Water bottle optional
Restrooms	Restroom with drinking water at Big Ring near the parking lot
Permits	None required
Area management	Washington State Parks and Recreation
Map	Washington State Parks
Season	Year-round

In the middle of the busy "east side" is a 482-acre, second-growth forest park crisscrossed with more than 28 miles of trail. Such a wonderful find so close to Interstate 405! The trails are well maintained, though often muddy in the winter. The terrain is gently sloped and the trails are wide. Except on the park's outside edges, you'd never know you weren't deep in the forest.

The land, a school trust property, was logged in 1880 to provide money for schools. Newcastle Trail went through this property connecting Redmond with the coal mines at Newcastle to the south. Logging and mining activity had stopped by the early 1930s, and an equestrian group transformed the skid roads into a network of riding trails. The Lake Washington Saddle Club has maintained the park since 1945, even though it is now a state park with a resident ranger. The Cascade Running Club hosts a 50K race here each January.

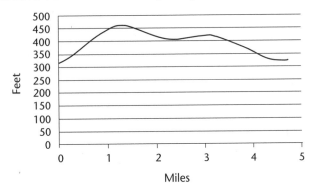

GETTING THERE

From Interstate 405 take Exit 17, which is just north of State Route 520. If approaching from the south, after the exit take an immediate right onto 116th Avenue. From the north, turn right onto 72nd Street

Sun through the trees at Bridle Trails

and go over the freeway. As 72nd turns into 70th, take the immediate right going south on 116th Avenue. Continue south to NE 53rd Street. The park entrance will be on your left. A large parking lot is to the right of the big horse ring.

THE RUN

Start with the 4.8-mile loop trail (the various trails here have no names) around the park's outer perimeter. Once you have a good sense of where you are in the park and how to navigate using the sounds of Interstate 405, feel free to explore within the park. A straight, gravel road under the powerlines can help you to get your bearings. The powerline divides the park into east-west sectors. The perimeter trail is the easiest to follow, but in the winter the interior trails are a little less muddy.

The 4.8-mile loop starts at the shelter by a big horse ring (A). There are toilets with running water and a pay phone at this location. The big ring hosts some very popular equestrian events most summer weekends. From the shelter, head out the driveway and take the trail to the right. This trail has gradual climbs as it heads north through the woods paralleling 116th Avenue NE.

In 0.4 mile the trail turns to the east (B). The hill here has one of the few 50-foot rises on the perimeter trail. The trail generally heads east for the next mile, following NE 60th Street at times while skirting residential areas. To follow the perimeter trail in a clockwise direction, stay to the left whenever a choice is offered and use the park boundary (sometimes fenced or a street) as your extreme left margin. At about 1.3 miles, you will come out to the powerline clearing and a smaller equestrian ring called Little Ring (C). Angle slightly to the right while crossing the powerline area, picking up the trail on the other side as it continues east. The trail will take a sharp right turn in the park's northeast corner (D). In a few minutes, take a quick left up the second 50-foot climb (E). The trail now parallels 132nd Avenue NE, which forms the park's eastern boundary. In 0.7 mile there is a sharp left (F), followed by a sharp right to keep you on the perimeter of the park. You'll see several stables (G) as you near the south end. Turn right and follow the gently sloping trail down through some chest-high brush. This is followed by several short climbs on the trail, which now heads west. Go straight across the powerline road and re-enter the trail. The trail again has a gentle downward slope in this area. Stay on this main trail and do not take the trails to the left. They lead out of the park into residential areas. In 0.4 mile you will intercept a wider trail (H). Turn left and follow this all the way to the parking area by the big ring. The increasing sound of Interstate 405 confirms that you are approaching the starting point.

SIGNIFICANT TRAIL LANDMARKS
A. Pick up the perimeter trail, going clockwise, at the big horse ring.
B. Trail turns right (east) at 0.4 mile.
C. Intersection with powerline clearing. Angle right to pick up trail across clearing.
D. Turn right at park's northeast corner.
E. Climb up a 50-foot hill.
F. At 2.5 miles you'll encounter a sharp left, then right on the perimeter path.
G. Horse stables. Turn right.
H. Intercept a wider trail at 4 miles. Turn left and follow this trail to the parking area.

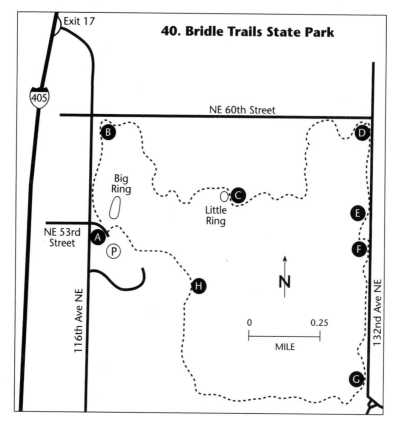

41 LAKE TO LAKE TRAIL

Distance	19 miles
Course geometry	Out and back
Running time	4.5 hours
Elevation gain	1500 feet
Highest altitude	340 feet
Difficulty	Easy
Water	Optional
Restrooms	Restrooms at Mercer Slough Winter House, Bellevue Botanical Gardens, Kelsey Creek Farm, Lake Hills Greenbelt Ranger Station, and Phantom Lake. All have drinking water.
Permits	None required
Area management	Bellevue Department of Parks and Recreation
Map	Bellevue Department of Parks and Recreation
Season	Year-round

Rather than just one trail, this is really a network of trails—part of my never-ending quest to travel through urban areas on trails. The Bellevue Parks Department has done a wonderful job of helping to make this possible. This route goes through a patchwork of parks, greenbelts, and some road from Lake Washington to Lake Sammamish. It is a wonderful way to appreciate the parks and waterways of Bellevue without waiting in traffic. The route is well maintained and well marked, though portions of it drop onto road for a few blocks here and there to get to the next park or greenbelt. This is a great trail for beginners, as trail shoes and water bottles are not required. Many miles of trail within each of the parks allow for shorter runs.

This area is rich in history, starting with Salish Indian villages on the east shore of Lake Washington, continuing to ownership of the Mercer Slough area by Aaron Mercer, and then the lowering of Lake Washington for the ship canal in 1916–1917. Wilburton Hill Park was a logging and sawmill operation that had to close when the canal project made it impossible for the steamers to make it up the slough to the mill. Kelsey Creek Farm was an operating dairy until 1942, and the Lake Hills Greenbelt was established as a wildlife corridor from Larsen Lake to Phantom Lake. This same corridor is said to have been part of an Indian trail traveling east from Lake Washington to near Fall City and over Naches Pass to Yakima. These areas were either donated to or purchased by the Bellevue Parks Department. Most of the parks along the way have a few additional miles of trail within them. For excellent information on the historical and current highlights of these parklands see another Mountaineers book, *Nature Walks In and Around Seattle.*

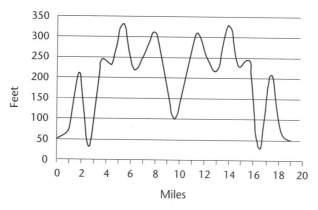

GETTING THERE

Going south from Interstate 405 in Bellevue, take the SE 8th Street exit and head west. Turn left onto 112th Avenue SE and continue to a left onto Bellevue Way SE. Park at the South Bellevue Park & Ride. The trail starts at the southwest corner of the Park & Ride.

Trail leading out of Kelsey Creek Park

THE RUN

Starting from the Park & Ride, head south along the Lake to Lake Trail (A). The trail is marked with 6-by-6-inch posts topped with blue-and-white signs. The signs generally have an arrow pointing to the next destination. Follow a boardwalk (B) east as it parallels Interstate 90 then head north (C) along the east perimeter of Mercer Slough Nature Park toward central Bellevue. Cross under Interstate 405 on SE 8th Street (D), then follow the signs up the hill to Wilburton Hill Park and the Bellevue Arboretum (E). The segment from Mercer Slough to Wilburton Hill Park is my least favorite part of the route because of its proximity to the highways. It gets better.

Pass by the information center in the arboretum, cross the parking lot, and pick up the Lake to Lake Trail as it leaves the arboretum across the park road and south of the ballpark (F). Wind down switchbacks until you're dumped out on 128th Avenue NE (G). Follow the signs along SE 4th Place to Kelsey Creek Park. Go straight through the park (unless you want a 2-mile detour to look at the animals and barns), cross the creek, and follow the signs to Lake Hills Greenbelt (H). When you emerge onto a gravel path under the powerlines (I), turn left (north) and then right on the wooden stairs through a residential area. You pass an exquisite terraced vegetable garden and come out onto SE 5th Street (J). Turn right at the outlet and go along SE 8th Street. At 148th Avenue NE, cross the road and enter the blueberry fields and Larsen Lake Park (K). Follow the signs to the Lake Hills Greenbelt Ranger Station, past a produce stand, and across 156th Avenue NE (L). Next follow the signs to Phantom Lake. Take the trail around Phantom Lake (M) as it curves northeast adjacent to a park on the north side of SE 16th Street before continuing east to 168th Avenue SE and Weowna Park. Turn right (south) along the west edge of Weowna Park (N) and continue for 0.5 mile. The trail turns east at this location and goes down along Phantom Creek to Lake Sammamish Parkway (O).

Most of the Lake Sammamish shoreline is privately owned. To get to Lake Sammamish, go down the hill from Weowna Park and cross West Lake Sammamish Parkway SE (O). Cross the parkway here if you need to touch the lake. An alternate road route is to continue past Phantom Lake on 156th Avenue SE, then take a left on 24th to West Lake Sammamish Parkway SE, where there is 126 feet of undeveloped shoreline open to the public. Better yet, look at the water from Weowna Park and consider that you've reached Lake Sammamish. The return route through the blueberry farm (P) can be very confusing. Follow the signs that point to 148th Avenue NE and head back the way you came.

The segment of trail from Wilburton Hill Park to Phantom Lake is the nicest section, with few road segments between parks. I frequently run this trail while my car is being serviced in Bellevue. The Bellevue Parks Department will provide a map of this route if you call them at 425-452-4109.

SIGNIFICANT TRAIL LANDMARKS

A. Go south out of the Park & Ride on the Lake to Lake Trail.
B. Take the boardwalk east as it parallels Interstate 90.
C. Turn left (north) along the park perimeter.
D. Cross under Interstate 405 on SE 8th Street.
E. Wilburton Hill Park and Bellevue Arboretum. Enter and head south.
F. Pass information center, cross parking lot, and follow trail east past ballfields and out of arboretum.
G. 128th Avenue NE. Follow signs to Kelsey Creek Park.
H. Go straight through Kelsey Creek Park and follow signs to Lake Hills Greenbelt.
I. A gravel path leads under powerlines at 6.3 mile. Turn left, then right up stairs through residential area.

J.   Trail comes out on SE 5th Street. Go straight, following Lake to Lake signs onto SE 8th Street.

K.   At 148th Avenue NE, enter blueberry fields and Larsen Lake Park.

L.   Cross 156th Avenue NE near a fruit and flower stand, headed toward Lake Hills Greenbelt Ranger Station.

M.   Take the trail around Phantom Lake.

N.   Turn right onto 168th Avenue SE at Weowna Park.

O.   Trail follows Phantom Creek east to West Lake Sammamish Parkway.

P.   Pass through blueberry fields, following signs to 148th Avenue NE, then return the way you came.

42 POINT DEFIANCE PARK

Distance	9.3 miles
Course geometry	Loop
Running time	2 hours
Elevation gain	200 feet
Highest altitude	200 feet
Difficulty	Easy
Water	Optional
Restrooms	Toilets and drinking fountains throughout the park
Permits	None required
Area management	Metro Parks Tacoma
Map	Available at the park or on the Metro Parks Tacoma website at *www.tacomaparks.com*
Season	Year-round

Point Defiance Park offers more than 20 miles of wide, well-marked trails through old-growth forest and along a bluff overlooking Puget Sound. There are few obstacles, so trail shoes are not required. The hills are not steep or long and there is no need to carry water, making this the perfect trail for the new trail runner.

Touted as the best and largest urban park in the Northwest, Point Defiance Park was originally reserved for military use but was never used for military operations. Point Defiance became a park in 1888 and occupies nearly 700 forested acres of peninsula and bluff, jutting northwesterly into Puget Sound. The two main trails parallel a 5-mile scenic drive that meanders through old-growth forests of fir, hemlock, and cedar, and past giant native rhododendrons reaching 15 feet or more in height. The perimeter route opens onto sweeping vistas of Puget Sound and the islands offshore.

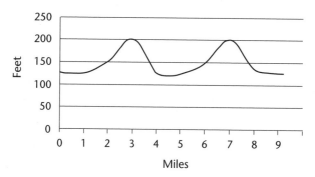

GETTING THERE

From Interstate 5 at Tacoma take State Route 16, Exit 132, toward the Narrows Bridge. Exit onto 6th Avenue and turn right onto State Route 164, Pearl Street. The Pearl Street entrance to the park is at 5400 North Pearl Street. Follow the park road around the rose garden and pagoda building and proceed to the second parking area just across from the lower zoo habitats. There is a restroom at the northwest end of this parking lot.

THE RUN

From the parking lot, head up Five-Mile Drive a quarter mile to the Rhododendron Garden (A). The three primary trails start here. The trails are well marked with signs designating the trails with a circle (Spine Trail), a triangle (Inside Perimeter Trail), and a square (Outside Perimeter Trail). The Spine Trail bisects the park peninsula and acts as the common starting point for the two perimeter trails. Go counterclockwise on these trails to see the views as ordered.

To begin, climb up the slight hill of the Spine Trail (circle) and take the Inside Perimeter Trail (triangle) where it branches off Spine. The Inside Perimeter Trail winds around the park peninsula, passing through large stands of old-growth trees as well as pruned salmonberry vines and salal brush. At times, a canopy of this natural shrubbery covers the trail. The Inside Perimeter Trail is a 4.5-mile loop, starting and ending at the Rhododendron Garden (A).

For the next loop, head back up the Spine Trail (circle), but this time take the Outside Perimeter Trail (square). At 1.25 miles (B) the

View from Gig Harbor Viewpoint

trail opens to a sweeping view of Colvos Passage (West Passage) and the southern end of Vashon Island. During salmon season, you might find a sea of fishing boats below. One-third mile farther is the Mountaineer Tree (C), one of the park's old-growth firs estimated to be more than 440 years old. Mountaineer Tree is 218 feet tall and 24 feet in circumference. The trail continues on to the Dalco Passage (D) and Gig Harbor (E) viewpoints. The Gig Harbor viewpoint, on the large bluff at the western extremity of the park, offers spectacular views toward Gig Harbor and the Olympic Mountains beyond. From the viewpoint, head left on the Five-Mile Drive a short distance until the trail resumes (F), heading toward the Narrows Bridge viewpoints. The trail gradually climbs, passing between Never Never Land, which is a nursery rhyme theme park, and Fort Nisqually, an 1800s Hudson Bay fort that was rebuilt here and includes some of the original buildings (G). After a short, steep descent, cross the park road (H) as the trail continues to the east before making sharp turns back toward the Rhododendron Garden. The Outer Perimeter Trail is 4.8 miles.

Three other trails can be added to the loops for variety. They are also marked with squares. The East and West Fort Nisqually Cross Trails have red squares and are short trails connecting the Inside Perimeter Trail to Spine Trail. A green square marks the quarter-mile trail (I) leading to the beach below the Mountaineer Tree.

SIGNIFICANT TRAIL LANDMARKS

A. Rhododendron Garden on Five-Mile Drive. Three trails start from here. Take Spine Trail (circle) to Inside Perimeter Trail (triangle). Go counterclockwise.

B. Vashon Island viewpoint from Outside Perimeter Trail (square).

C. Mountaineer Tree. Continue on Outside Perimeter Trail (square).

D. Pass Dalco Passage viewpoint.

E. Pass Gig Harbor viewpoint. Head left on Five-Mile Drive for a short distance.

F. Circle and square trails converge. Go right on the square Outside Perimeter Trail.

G. Never Never Land and Fort Nisqually. Continue through.

H. Cross park road and head back to Rhododendron Garden.

I. A 0.25-mile trail to the beach (green).

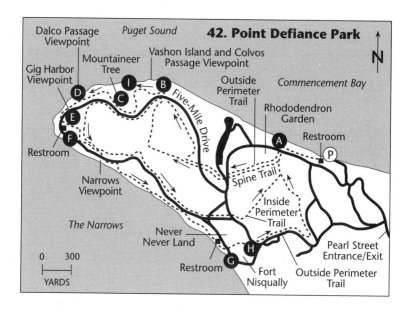

43 SNOQUALMIE VALLEY

Distance	18.8 miles
Course geometry	Point to point
Running time	3 hours
Elevation gain	1400 feet
Highest altitude	490 feet
Difficulty	Easy
Water	40 ounces
Restrooms	Outhouse at McCormick Park, Nick Loutsis Park
Permits	None required
Area management	King County Parks
Map	King County Parks website at *www.metrokc.gov/parks/*
Season	Year-round

Care to run from Duvall to Snoqualmie Falls? The Snoqualmie Valley Trail is the perfect route. Traveling along a gradually ascending former railroad grade, it follows the Snoqualmie River through the farmland and small towns of the Snoqualmie Valley. It is entirely runnable and partially shady. The surface is a mix of dirt and gravel and is suitable for road shoes. At the time of publication, the trail is only contiguous from the Woodinville–Duvall Road to the Tokul Tunnel, almost 19 miles. With a couple miles of road in between, the trail can be rejoined at Mount Si Golf Course where it continues to Rattlesnake Lake.

GETTING THERE
From Interstate 405 near Woodinville, take Exit 23a to State Route 522. Take the second exit (195th Street) off State Route 522. Turn right.

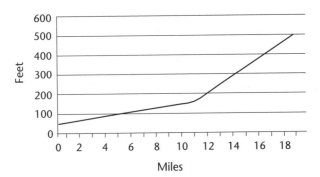

Drive 10 miles, cross the Snoqualmie River, and turn right on the main street through Duvall (State Route 203). The trail access areas can all be reached from this road. Several parking areas on unmarked side streets are depicted on the accompanying map. There may be signs for McCormick Park and Duvall Park, which is within 1 mile of the Snoqualmie River bridge, but they are not well marked at this writing. Turn right on NE Stephens Street to reach McCormick Park. To make the trip official, you can run north to the Woodinville–Duvall bridge before heading south.

THE RUN

Entering the Snoqualmie Valley Trail at Duvall near McCormick Park (A), head south along the Snoqualmie River and wetlands. One side of the road will have crops and pasture, the other wetlands. The trail curves away from the highway. Cement bridges span any non-runnable areas. As you approach the town of Carnation, the trail crosses Highway 203 (B). Shortly after the road crossing is Nick Loutsis Park (Entwhistle Street) (C). There is a portable toilet here and a water pump.

Tokul tunnel

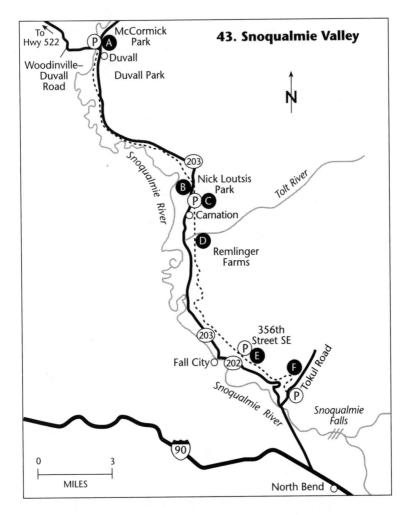

The trail crosses the wide Tolt River on a footbridge (D), then passes Remlinger Farms. The trail goes from a 10-feet-per-mile ascent to a 50-feet-per-mile ascent and heads inland toward Fall City. The last convenient access point to this trail is at 356th Street, which is about 0.4 mile from Highway 203 east of its intersection with Highway 202 (E). The trail currently ends at Tokul Tunnel (F), but signs of construction suggest the trail is being expanded. It is nearly impossible to get lost on this trail. A car can be left at each end of the trail for a one-way run. You can even choose whether you want to run a gradual up or a gradual down.

SIGNIFICANT TRAIL LANDMARKS

A. Enter Snoqualmie Valley Trail near McCormick Park. Go left on the trail.

B. Trail crosses State Route 203 at 7.5 miles. Pick up trail on the other side.

C. The Nick Loutsis Park, which has a water pump and a portable toilet.

D. Footbridge over Tolt River at 9.3 miles.

E. The most eastward trail access to the trail is 356th Street. It has convenient parking.

F. Tokul Tunnel. Return the way you came.

ISSAQUAH ALPS

Although Cougar, Squak, and Tiger Mountains are often referred to as foothills of the Cascades, many geologists claim that they are part of an older range called the Issaquah Alps.

Cougar Mountain is the westernmost of the three and closest to Seattle, Bellevue, Issaquah, and the suburbs for a nice after-work run. Squak Mountain seems squished between Cougar and Tiger Mountains and has steeper but shorter trails than the other two. Tiger Mountain is a favorite training place for most of the greater Seattle trail runners. It has all the diversity a trail runner needs for any kind of run. There are steep climbs, technical ascents, beautiful views, and long runnable segments on more than 100 miles of deep forest trail. Most of the trails are closed to wheeled vehicles, though some trails are declared multi-use for part of the year.

Tiger Mountain has three major peaks: West (2948 feet in elevation), East (3004 feet), and South (2026 feet), with minor peaks West Tiger No. 2 (2757 feet in elevation) and West Tiger No. 3 (2522 feet).

A network of abandoned logging railroad grades from the mills at Hobart, High Point, and Preston form the foundation of the Tiger Mountain trail system. These were used during the last third of the 19th century until sometime in the 1920s when truck-logging roads were added. The west side of Tiger Mountain was mostly logged using trucks, and the grades are steeper than the rest of Tiger. The east side of Tiger has a lot of switchback trails where the trains pushed and pulled themselves up the side of the mountain. During the Depression, the railroad loggers decided it was not worth it anymore and picked up their rails and ties and left.

The mountain has since undergone private ownership and trail activities of all kinds. By 1980 there was a land exchange with the State Department of Natural Resources that converted Tiger Mountain to a working state forest and left the private owner with only the lucrative communication tower colonies on the peaks of West and East Tiger. Tiger is still a working forest but has become a model for kinder, gentler forestry techniques.

44 COUGAR MOUNTAIN RING

Distance	14 miles
Course geometry	Loop
Running time	3.75 hours
Elevation gain	2200 feet
Highest altitude	1595 feet
Difficulty	Moderate
Water	40 ounces, spring-fed water supply (halfway)
Restrooms	Outhouse at trailhead
Permits	None required
Area management	Department of Natural Resources (DNR)
Map	DNR Tiger Mountain, Squak Mountain, Cougar Mountain, Tradition Plateau (all in one map)
Season	Year-round

The Cougar Mountain Ring or Grand Tour, as it has been referred to, has many variations. This route starts from the Wilderness Creek Trailhead and begins with a quick climb through a heavily forested area to the highest point on Cougar Mountain Regional and Wildland Park. The route is classified as moderate, but provides a good workout for the advanced trail runner as well. The many trails of Cougar Mountain have much history associated with them. Fred's Railroad Trail was named for Fred Round, who was known for his mining activities in the 1920s and lived his whole life on Cougar Mountain. Harvey Manning, a prolific author of several essential guidebooks to the Northwest, named Shy Bear Trail for the bear that spent much of the winter sleeping at the Shy Bear Bivouac junction with Wilderness Peak Trail. The bear was heard, but never seen. During visits to Cougar Mountain, the bears we named Huckleberry or Blackberry for their incomplete digestion have never shown themselves. Are they descendants of Shy Bear?

Don't let the excess of trail names discourage you. The trails are well marked and the various segments are short.

GETTING THERE

Take Exit 15 off Interstate 90 near Issaquah and go south on State Route 900 (Renton–Issaquah Road SE). It is 2.5 miles to the Wilderness Creek Trailhead on your right. The trailhead parking is limited, so if you are running with others consider using the Issaquah Park & Ride two blocks off Interstate 90 along SR 900, 2 miles away.

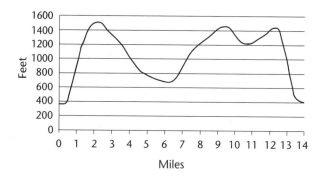

THE RUN

The Wilderness Creek Trail crosses the creek within 200 feet of the trailhead (A) and begins the climb up along the creek. The trail is initially rocky and passes under large trees. This area of Cougar Mountain was too remote for railroad logging in the 1920s. Later logging also bypassed the Wilderness Creek area because of the steep slopes. The Wilderness Cliffs Trail intersects at 0.6 mile (B). Turn right and follow the Wilderness Cliffs Trail to Cougar Mountain's high point of Wilderness Peak (1595 feet) in 1.3 miles (C). From the viewpoint, it is another 0.5 mile (the trail is now called Wilderness Peak Trail) past the Shy Bear Trail and straight across the intersection to a right onto the Long View Peak Trail. Once you are off the Wilderness trails, the rest of Cougar Mountain's trails traverse shorter, rolling hills.

Long View Peak is the second highest point on Cougar Mountain at 1445 feet in elevation. The view looks south toward May Creek Valley. The Long View Peak Trail turns into Deceiver Trail (D) after passing the high point. The 1.2-mile Deceiver Trail was named by Ralph Owen, who partnered with Harvey Manning in exploring and naming many of the park's trails. Owen supposedly deceived his wife into an 8-hour trek to Long View Peak before there was a trail. Deceiver Trail connects to Shy Bear Trail (E), which then becomes the Far Country Trail. Turn left onto Shy Bear and continue straight onto Far Country. The Far Country Lookout is mostly overgrown and doesn't offer much of a vista. From the lookout, the trail switchbacks down to the Indian Trail (F), which is 4.5 miles in. Go right. Indian Trail is very wide with a slight slope. It is easy to pick up the pace here.

Just past an intersection with Quarry Trail, Indian Trail becomes Red Town Trail (G). Not too long after, there is a wooden pipe supplying fresh spring water. This is at 6.5 miles. Fill your water bottles here if needed, and you will have enough for the remainder of the loop. Numerous abandoned coal mine shafts can be seen off of the Red Town Trail. Just 0.2 mile from the Red Town trailhead (H), turn right (east) onto the Cave Hole Trail and follow it 1.2 miles to the Clay Pit Road (I). The continuation of the trail on the other side of Clay Pit Road is called Coyote Creek Trail. Follow Coyote for approximately 0.7 mile to a right run onto the Klondike Swamp Trail (J). After 0.1 mile, turn left onto the Lost Beagle Trail (Ralph Owen, of Deceiver Trail fame, is credited with building the trail and then losing his beagle here for 3 days) and follow it west to a sharp right turn onto Anti-Aircraft Ridge Trail (K). Stands of alder and fir trees in this area hide almost all signs of earlier logging activity.

At 1430 feet in elevation, Anti-Aircraft Peak is the third highest point on the mountain. There are large grassy knolls and open areas for those

Crossing a wooden bridge near the Cougar Mountain trailhead

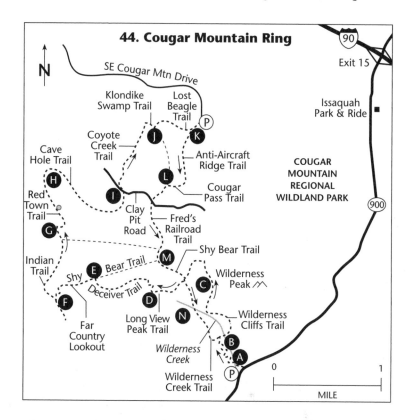

44. Cougar Mountain Ring

N

SE Cougar Mtn Drive

Klondike Swamp Trail
Lost Beagle Trail
P

Coyote Creek Trail

J

K

Cave Hole Trail

H

Anti-Aircraft Ridge Trail

L

Cougar Pass Trail

Red Town Trail

I

G

Clay Pit Road

Fred's Railroad Trail

Indian Trail

Shy Bear Trail

M

Shy Bear Trail

E

Wilderness Peak

Deceiver Trail

F

D

N

C

Far Country Lookout

Long View Peak Trail

Wilderness Cliffs Trail

Wilderness Creek

B

A

Wilderness Creek Trail

P

90

Exit 15

Issaquah Park & Ride

COUGAR MOUNTAIN REGIONAL WILDLAND PARK

900

0   1

MILE

who want to drive there for picnics. But if you don't like witnessing rapid development of recently forested areas, don't drive to Anti-Aircraft Peak to start your run.

The Anti-Aircraft Ridge Trail heads south for 0.7 mile through more alder and fir to Cougar Pass Trail at 10.5 miles. Turn left. Go 0.2 mile farther and turn left back onto the Klondike Swamp Trail (L). When the Klondike Swamp Trail meets the Clay Pit Road, it becomes Fred's Railroad Trail. The trail in this section often goes over broken bricks and evidence of the clay deposits in the area around the privately owned clay pit. Follow Fred's Railroad Trail south for 0.6 mile until it intersects the Quarry Trail and the Shy Bear Trail (M), both in less than 0.1 mile. Take a left (southeast) onto Shy Bear to return back to Wilderness Creek Trail (N). From the Wilderness Creek Trail (you've now run 12.4 miles), it is an easy 1.6-mile run back down to the trailhead and completion of this version of the Cougar Mountain Ring.

SIGNIFICANT TRAIL LANDMARKS

A. Wilderness Creek trailhead. Trail crosses creek within 200 feet.

B. Go right on Wilderness Cliffs Trail.

C. Cougar Mountain high point. Trail becomes Wilderness Peak Trail.

D. Go right onto Long View Peak Trail, which becomes Deceiver Trail. Continue straight.

E. Go left onto Shy Bear Trail, which becomes Far Country Trail.

F. Go right on Indian Trail down the switchbacks.

G. Indian Trail becomes Red Town Trail after you pass Quarry Trail. Natural spring soon follows.

H. Turn right onto Cave Hole Trail.

I. Clay Pit Road. Cross road to pick up trail, now called Coyote Creek Trail.

J. Go left on Klondike Swamp Trail, then right on Lost Beagle Trail.

K. At 9.4 miles take a sharp right onto Anti-Aircraft Ridge Trail.

L. Go left onto Cougar Pass Trail, then take another left onto Klondike Swamp Trail.

M. Go left on Shy Bear Trail to return to Wilderness Creek Trail and the parking lot.

N. Follow Wilderness Creek Trail to trailhead and parking.

The author nears the end of the Cougar Mountain run.

45 SQUAK MOUNTAIN

Distance	8 miles
Course geometry	Loop
Running time	2 hours
Elevation gain	1680 feet
Highest altitude	2020 feet
Difficulty	Moderate
Water	40 ounces
Restrooms	None at trailhead. Restroom at south entrance off May Valley Road
Permits	None required
Area management	Department of Natural Resources (DNR)
Map	DNR Tiger Mountain, Squak Mountain, Cougar Mountain, Tradition Plateau (all in one map)
Season	Year-round

Well maintained and well marked, Squak Mountain is a good intermediate trail. The close proximity to Issaquah makes it an urban wilderness that is especially good for an evening run after work. Since there hasn't been any logging on Squak Mountain for more than fifty years, there are limited "peek-a-boo" views of Tiger Mountain, Issaquah, and Lake Sammamish. For a small area, Squak Mountain has many trails. Like many of the intermediate trails described in this book, Squak is a good workout for an advanced runner looking for a short but brisk run.

Squak Mountain got its name from the Native American term for the fertile valley, creek, and mountain that now form the town of Issaquah. Geologically, Squak Mountain is the middle or "little sister" in the Cougar, Squak, and Tiger Mountain threesome, commonly known as the Issaquah Alps. Like the others, over the years Squak has been

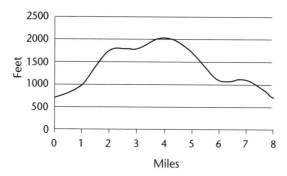

logged and was the site of a wooden tie mill and a coal mine. Starting in the 1940s, Seattle attorney Stinson Bullitt began acquiring the land and stopped any further commercial exploits. In 1972 his family (founders of KING radio and television) donated the land to the state with the stipulation that it would never be logged. Slowly, Squak Mountain State Park is returning to natural forest.

GETTING THERE

From Interstate 90 near Issaquah, take Exit 15 and go two blocks south on State Route 900, then turn left (east) onto Newport Way by the Issaquah Park & Ride. Take a right (south) on South 12th Avenue NW. Twelfth Avenue turns into Mt. Olympus Drive, then Mt. Olympus Drive SW. Mt. Olympus becomes Mt. Park Boulevard SW. About 1 mile beyond

Bullitt fireplace

Newport Way, turn right onto Mountainside Drive and continue up. After 0.2 mile Mountainside makes a sharp turn to the left and there is a slight extension of Idylwood Road straight ahead with a large rock community sign (no name) to the left. This is the parking area for the Mountainside Drive trailhead. Enter the trail straight ahead.

The newest trailhead for Squak Mountain is off of May Valley Road on the south side, complete with a solar restroom and large parking lot. At the time of this writing, not all of the trails leading from the south trailhead were complete.

THE RUN

The Bullitt Access Trail starts from the parking lot at 700 feet in elevation, with a gentle 300-foot climb. In 0.5 mile you reach the Coal Mine Trail (A). Take this trail straight ahead for 0.1 mile to an intersection with the West Access Peak Trail (B). Jog left on the West Access Peak Trail and then right on the Central Peak Trail to reach the Chybinski Trail in 0.2 mile (C). Go right. This trail provides a route to the south side of Squak Mountain and then back to the Bullitt Fireplace Trail (D). Turn right onto the Bullitt Fireplace Trail. This trail has many fallen alder and fir trees along it, adding a steeplechase challenge to the route. A climb to 1700 feet in elevation is followed by a quick, 200-foot drop before you finish climbing to the Bullitt fireplace. A large stone fireplace and a concrete slab are all that remain of the original dwelling.

From the fireplace to the summit, the trail is built on old rock smoothed over by erosion. A cluster of communication towers, not unlike the other Issaquah Alps mountaintops, crowns the summit (2020 feet in elevation). Continue over the summit on the Bullitt Fireplace Trail to a left onto the Summit Trail (E), which drops down to a left turn onto the Equestrian Trail. This is a rapid descent of 650 feet in a mile. The Equestrian Trail heads west along an abandoned logging grade, providing an occasional view through the trees toward Tiger Mountain and the city of Issaquah. At the Tie Mill (no longer apparent), a new trail drops down to the East Side Trail (F). Go left and follow the East Side Trail to the west. There are occasional bridges over small streams that generally have very little water flowing. Don't count on them for emergency drinking water. In this section there is a marker recognizing an Eagle Scout who worked on the trail in 1997. Continue for another mile beyond the marker to reach the Access Trail (G). Go right. It is 0.5 mile to another right turn onto the Bullitt Access Trail and back to the Mountainside Drive trailhead.

SIGNIFICANT TRAIL LANDMARKS

A. Take Bullitt Access Trail to Coal Mine Trail. Go straight ahead 0.1 mile.

B. Jog left onto West Access Peak Trail, then right onto Central Peak Trail.

C. Go right onto Chybinski Trail.

D. Go right onto Bullitt Fireplace Trail.

E. Cross summit at 3.7 miles then go left onto Summit Trail, which drops steeply to an equestrian trail. Turn left.

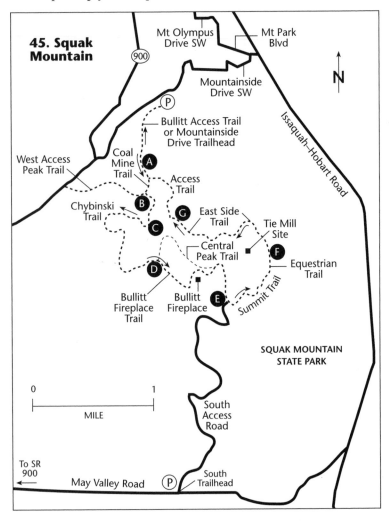

F.   New trail drops down to East Side Trail (may not be marked but
     if you look to the right, you'll see it). Go left on East Side Trail.
G.   Go right onto Access Trail for 0.5 mile to a right onto Bullitt
     Access Trail back to the trailhead.

46 TRADITION LAKE PLATEAU

Distance	6 miles
Course geometry	Loop
Running time	1.5 hours
Elevation gain	600 feet
Highest altitude	520 feet
Difficulty	Easy
Water	20 ounces
Restrooms	At parking lot, no water available
Permits	None required
Area management	Department of Natural Resources (DNR)
Maps	Issaquah Alps, Green Trails #204S
Season	Year-round

This pleasant loop on Tiger Mountain's Tradition Lake Plateau offers
fairly level, scenic trails with occasional rolling hills and one semi-long
climb. It has all the usual roots and rocks that a trail runner encounters,
providing a good introduction and good practice for the beginning trail
runner. It's close in to Seattle and Bellevue, and there is plenty of parking.

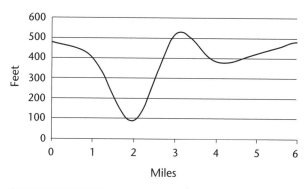

GETTING THERE
From Interstate 90 east of Issaquah, take Exit 20 (High Point). Turn
right on the frontage road and go 0.4 mile to the gate. If the gate is open

Tradition Lake

and you know you will be finished running before dusk, you may continue by car 0.5 mile to the upper parking lot; otherwise park outside the gate, which closes at dusk.

THE RUN

Head north from the parking lot toward the gate near the top of the access road. Pass through the log gate marked Swamp Trail (A). Follow the trail to the right through the damp forest past storyboards and over boardwalks that really do keep you out of the swamp. Swamp Trail empties into a powerline clearing where you turn right and run for a few feet to a sign marking the entrance to Brink Trail (B). Go left onto the trail. Note that two powerlines cross the Tradition Plateau: Puget Power's lines run east–west and Bonneville Power's lines run north–south. Brink Trail, which is nearly level, ends in 0.7 mile under the Puget Power lines. Turn right (west), follow the wide, flat trail, and look for a steeply descending dirt trail (C). The trail has a log entrance, but no name. You'll get some practice on steep downhills here. Continue in a switchback pattern down the hill. Take the right path of the first fork and the left path on the second. At the bottom (D), go straight on a scotch broom–lined trail—one map calls this the Issaquah Trail, but there is no sign. You'll come to the Issaquah High School gym. Turn left onto an unmarked trail directly across from the gym (E), then turn right almost immediately and head up the longish ascent (F). This trail is sometimes called Issaquah Trail and sometimes High School Trail, since the sign at the top has an arrow on the trail pointing toward the high school. Just before a wide spot in the trail (generally a huge mud puddle), turn left at the log gate onto the trail marked Adventure (G). This thickly forested trail is across rolling hills and gives a good feel for trail running without the quad-killing steep ascents. Continue on

Adventure Trail for 0.9 mile until you pass the Puget Power line and get back onto Brink Trail (C). This time, take a right onto Big Tree Trail (H) and see the last remaining trees of the never-logged forest. When coming out of Big Tree, take a right (south) on the Bonneville Power Trail (I) and follow it east to Tradition Lake, then enter the Around the Lake Trail (J). This trail leads back to the parking lot. To see the other side of the lake, continue around on the Puget Power Trail, looping around the lake one and a half times, and join the Around the Lake Trail until you are back at the parking lot.

SIGNIFICANT TRAIL LANDMARKS

A. Entrance to Swamp Trail. Go right (north).
B. Powerline clearing. Go right for entrance to Brink Trail. Go left (west) onto the trail.
C. Brink Trail ends under powerlines. Go right on gravel trail and look for an unmarked trail going steeply downhill.
D. Continue straight at bottom of the hill.
E. Go left (east) on unmarked trail across from high school gym.
F. Take an immediate right onto High School or Issaquah Trail.
G. Go left onto Adventure Trail to return to Brink Trail.
H. Take a right onto Big Tree Trail.
I. Turn right onto Bonneville Power Trail. Follow to Tradition Lake.
J. Enter the Around the Lake Trail from Puget Powerline Road. Go right (south, then east) to return to parking lot.

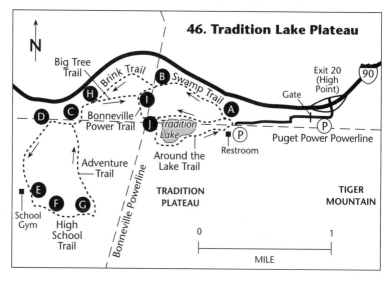

46. Tradition Lake Plateau

47 TWELVE SUMMITS

Distance	34 miles
Course geometry	Out and back, with possible variations
Running time	11 hours
Elevation gain	10,500 feet
Highest altitude	3004 feet
Difficulty	Strenuous
Water	60 ounces, water treatment supplies, and leave reserve water at South Tiger Mountain trailhead if possible
Restrooms	Outhouse at High Point trailhead
Permits	None required
Area management	Department of Natural Resources (DNR)
Maps	Tiger Mountain Trails, Issaquah Alps Trail Club (Guide to Trails of Tiger Mountain), Green Trails Maps #204S, Tiger Mountain Map, DNR Washington State
Season	Year-round

This is a tough and wonderful training run for mountainous 100-mile races. It will also impress your friends. Traveling over six summits and doubling back over them in 34 miles gives the experience of long climbs on tired legs. Make sure you have enough daylight for the trip, and plan to be out before your car is locked behind the High Point parking lot gate (times posted at gate). Scott Jurek, who won the 1999, 2000, and 2001 Western States 100 Endurance Run, uses this route to train. With a car stationed near the South Tiger Mountain trailhead you could do 17 miles and six summits, still a formidable task, but you would miss

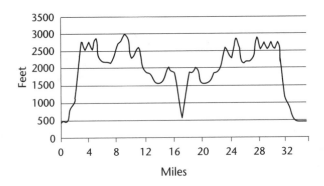

the incredible climb up the back side of Middle Tiger. Take the map and the list of trails under Significant Trail Landmarks.

GETTING THERE

From Interstate 90 east of Issaquah, take Exit 20 (High Point). Turn right on the frontage road and go 0.4 mile to the gate. If the gate is open and you know you will be finished running before dusk, you may continue by car 0.5 mile to the upper parking lot; otherwise park outside the gate, which closes at dusk.

To leave water at the South Tiger Mountain trailhead for use on your return trip, take Exit 15 from Interstate 90, head south, and turn left onto Newport Way just past the Park & Ride (Newport Way becomes the Issaquah–Hobart Road). You can also take State Route 18 and turn north onto Issaquah–Hobart Road. From either direction, turn onto Tiger Mountain Road SE. Tiger Mountain Road SE forms a semicircle off Issaquah–Hobart Road. The trailhead is next to a SCHOOL BUS STOP AHEAD sign on the south end of the road.

Going to East Tiger Mountain

THE RUN

From the upper parking lot, take the West Tiger No. 3 Trail (A) south to a right turn onto the Bus Trail (B). Follow Bus to a left onto the Nook Trail (C) and then a short section on the Nook Connector Trail (D). The connector comes to an intersection with the Section Line Trail (E). Go left. Section Line takes a direct route (up and up and up) to the summit of West Tiger No. 3 (F) (elevation 2522 feet). Go over the bare summit and down switchbacks on the south side as you head south toward the summit of West Tiger No. 2 (G) (elevation 2757 feet).

From West Tiger No. 2, follow the steep Main Tiger Mountain Road down around a vehicle gate (H) and then up to the summit of West Tiger No. 1 (I) (elevation 2948 feet). A hikers' hut here signals the entrance to the Non-Ionizing Electromagnetic Radiation (NIER) Bypass Trail that skirts the high electric fields of the communication towers. Follow the signs to Bootleg Trail (J) and take Bootleg in an easterly direction downhill. At the bottom of the hill, take two quick trails that veer to the right to put you on the railroad grade, which is a fairly flat, wide trail (K). In 0.1 mile turn left on the East Tiger Trail (L). The sign for this trail is periodically missing.

The East Tiger Trail follows an old logging grade in places as it moves through a dense fir forest. Cross the Preston Railroad grade (M)

Black bear paw print along the salmonberry bushes on South Tiger Mountain

and continue 0.5 mile until the trail ends at a log gate and dumps you onto East Side Road (N). Go right on East Side Road a short distance up the hill to the manmade structure at the lookout of East Tiger Summit (O) (elevation 3004 feet). Turn around and head back down East Side Road, passing East Tiger Trail, and taking a right on Crossover Road to connect with Main Tiger Mountain Road (P). Follow Tiger Mountain Road 1.1 miles. Turn left and head southwesterly on a logging road (Q). There is a turnaround area at the end of this road. On the left (east) side of the turnaround is the entrance to Middle Tiger Trail leading to the Middle Tiger Summit (R) (elevation 2607 feet).

Continue on the steep Middle Tiger Trail as it heads south to cross the Tiger Mountain Trail (TMT) (S). Keep going on Middle Tiger Trail down to an intersection with West Side Road (T). Go left. You also have an option of turning left on the TMT instead of crossing it. The West Side Road provides more climb and brings you back to intersection with the TMT in 1.5 miles (U). Approaching from West Side Road, turn right through the vehicle gate to pick up the Tiger Mountain Trail. Proceed to a right turn onto South Tiger Traverse Logging Road until you come to the South Tiger Traverse Trail at the top of the hill (currently marked by a rock cairn) (V). Go right. Follow that trail until you see a huge stump with the appearance of eyes cut into it (W). Turn left at the stump and proceed to the summit of South Tiger Mountain (elevation 2028 feet) on the Nicholl South Tiger Mountain Trail. The trail was named for Ron Nicholl, who insists that you have to reach every summit. He made the now-famous trail during his recovery from first bushwhacking his way in, falling in a hole, wrenching his back across a log, and hyperextending his knee. There is a logbook hidden under a rock near the USGS marker. Sign in if you like; the logbook was put there by a Green River Community College survey class.

Return to the South Tiger Traverse, heading left and down for longer than you ever thought possible. When the berries are ripe in the spring and summer, you may see bear paw prints on this route. Join the TMT (X) for the last 1.3 miles to the south trailhead and on to Tiger Mountain Road (Y), where you may have left fresh supplies. Turn around here and go back the way you came or get in your second car and go home.

The return trip over the six summits follows the same route, but it seems quite different as you climb trails that didn't seem nearly so long on the descent. Following the West Tiger No. 3 Trail all the way on the final descent seems faster and easier, but hikers and families with children and pets also frequent it. If your quads feel strong enough, you can opt for the free-fall descent of taking the Section Line Trail followed by the Nook Connector and Nook Trail, then the Bus Trail to the parking lot. There are rarely tourists on this route.

SIGNIFICANT TRAIL LANDMARKS

A.   Follow West Tiger No. 3 Trail south out of the parking lot.

B.   Turn right onto Bus Trail.

C.   Turn left onto Nook Trail and start the ascent.

D.   Nook Connector Trail comes in at 1.9 miles. Go right.

E.   Go left onto Section Line Trail.

F.   West Tiger Mountain 3 summit. Trail continues down switchbacks on the south side.

G.   West Tiger Mountain 2 summit. Follow Main Tiger Mountain Road toward West Tiger No. 1.

H.   Go around gate on Main Tiger Mountain Road.

I.   West Tiger No. 1 summit is at 5.2 miles. Pick up the NIER Bypass Trail next to the hikers' hut.

J.   Follow Bootleg Trail easterly downhill.

K.   At bottom of hill, take two quick rights turn right onto railroad grade.

L.   Go left on East Tiger Trail.

M.   Cross Preston Railroad grade.

N.   Turn right onto East Side Road up to the summit of East Tiger Mountain.

O.   East Tiger summit. Turn around and follow East Side Road to Crossover Road. Turn right onto road.

P.   Go right on Main Tiger Mountain Road. Continue for 1.1 miles.

Q.   At 11.5 miles head southwest on a logging road.

R.   Near the end of the logging road, enter Middle Tiger Trail leading to the summit of Middle Tiger Mountain.

S.   Cross Tiger Mountain Trail on Middle Tiger Mountain Trail.

T.   Go left onto West Side Road, follow for 1.5 miles, and then turn through vehicle gate.

U.   Intersection of West Side Road and Tiger Mountain Trail. Go right onto trail.

V.   Go right on South Tiger Traverse Logging Road and then right again onto South Tiger Traverse Trail.

W.   Turn left at stump onto Nicholl South Tiger Mountain Trail. Return to South Tiger Traverse and head down.

X.   Join the Tiger Mountain Trail, heading south.

Y.   South trailhead. Retrieve second car here or retrieve water and turn around to return the way you came.

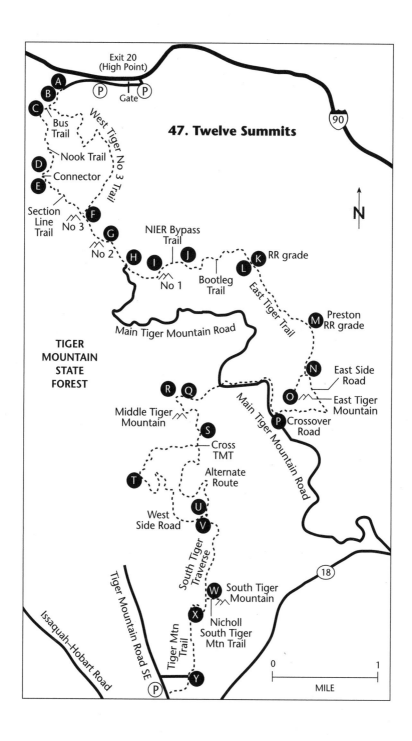

Exit 20
(High Point)

(P) Gate (P)

A
B
C

Bus
Trail

Nook Trail

West Tiger No 3 Trail

D
Connector
E

Section
Line
Trail

No 3

F

G

No 2

H   I   J

No 1

NIER Bypass
Trail

Bootleg
Trail

K   RR grade
L

East Tiger Trail

M   Preston
RR grade

N   East Side
Road

O   East Tiger
Mountain

P   Crossover
Road

R   Q

Middle Tiger
Mountain

S

Cross
TMT

T

Alternate
Route

West
Side Road

U
V

South Tiger Traverse

Main Tiger Mountain Road

Main Tiger Mountain Road

TIGER
MOUNTAIN
STATE
FOREST

N

47. Twelve Summits

90

18

W   South Tiger
Mountain

X   Nicholl
South Tiger
Mtn Trail

Tiger Mtn Trail

Tiger Mountain Road SE

Issaquah–Hobart Road

Y

(P)

0   1

MILE

48 THREE SUMMITS

Distance	10 miles
Course geometry	Loop
Running time	2.5 hours
Elevation gain	3500 feet
Highest altitude	2948 feet
Difficulty	Strenuous
Water	40 ounces
Area management	Department of Natural Resources (DNR)
Maps	DNR Tiger Mountain Map, Issaquah Alps Tiger Mountain Map, Green Trails #204S
Season	Year-round, occasional snow on top in winter

This route offers a variety of trail running experiences, from rapid ascents to technical descents. The steep Section Line Trail is a great place to practice a climbing walk. A very slow but steady walk up this grade can result in a heart rate equal to running on other trails. Poo Top is a very technical trail with many short, descending turns through the trees. One View and Poo Poo Point Trails are also tricky but more open, allowing you to anticipate your movements. Adventure, Swamp, and Brink Trails are flatter but still provide the challenge of irregular terrain. This is an excellent, 2.5-hour trail run for the advanced trail runner.

GETTING THERE

From Interstate 90 east of Issaquah, take Exit 20 (High Point). Turn right on the frontage road and go 0.4 mile to the gate. If the gate is open and you know you will be finished running before dusk, you may continue by car 0.5 mile to the upper parking lot; otherwise park outside the gate, which closes at dusk.

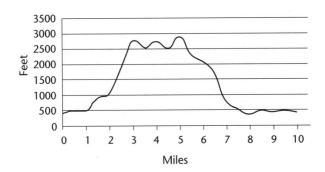

Bridge over the creek along the Bus Trail

THE RUN

From the upper parking lot, take the West Tiger No. 3 Trail (A) south to a right turn onto the Bus Trail (B). Follow it for about 500 feet to a left onto the Nook Trail (C). The trails are pretty well marked and many have log entrance chutes that prevent bikes and horses from getting through. The Nook Trail starts out with a gentle climb, then steepens along an old logging cable line. From Nook, take a right onto the Connector Trail over to the Section Line Trail (D). Go left. This trail boasts a lone Western white pine tree amongst the hemlock and fir, as well as an elevation gain of 2300 feet over 2.8 miles. Just when you think your quads are finished, you see what looks like a dirt road—you are at the summit of West Tiger No. 3 (elevation 2522 feet) (E). The view from here encompasses Mount Rainier to the south, the Olympic Mountains in the distance, Bellevue, Seattle, and Puget Sound. West Tiger No. 3 is the most popular destination for Tiger Mountain hikers, most of whom arrive via the West Tiger No. 3 Trail. Pause at the top to quiet the throbbing of your calves and quads; then take the short switchback south on the Section Line Trail to the saddle between the second and third summits and on up to West Tiger No. 2 (F) (elevation 2757 feet).

From the summit of West Tiger No. 2, follow the steep Main Tiger Mountain Road down, through a gate, and then back up to the summit of West Tiger No. 1 (G) (elevation 2948 feet). A hikers' hut here signals the entrance to the Non-Ionizing Electromagnetic Radiation (NIER) Bypass Trail that skirts the high electric fields of the communication towers. After about 0.4 mile, branch onto West Tiger No. 1 Trail, going steeply uphill (H). Cross a road to enter the Poo Top Trail (I). Take Poo Top Trail down to the Hidden Forest Trail and right onto the Tiger Mountain Trail (TMT) (J). Follow TMT (which at this point is a short segment connecting Hidden Forest Trail and One View Trail) to a left turn onto One View Trail (K). Whatever view was here when the trail was named seems to be hidden now. One View Trail connects with the Poo Poo Point Trail (L) as you continue to descend. The name Poo Poo came from Harvey Manning, the renowned hiking enthusiast, for the communication signal made between the logging yarder and the choker setter. They were often out of sight of each other, and the "poo poo" sound from the steam whistle would signify "all set." Farther down Poo Poo Point Trail, you'll find Gap Creek (M), spanned by a wood bridge built in 1997 to replace a rotted-out logging trestle. This is a year-round creek, in case you need emergency water. The water should be treated before drinking.

As you head down Poo Poo Point Trail toward Issaquah High School, you can rest assured that your hard work is done. Use the Tradition Lake Plateau area as a cool-down. The entrance to Adventure Trail is just beyond a big metal culvert (N). Adventure is a pleasantly forested, 0.9-mile trail with short, gentle hills. When emerging at the powerlines, go slightly down (straight) to Brink Trail (O). The sound of traffic on Interstate 90 gives assurance that you are on the correct route back to your starting point.

The Brink Trail continues 0.7 mile on the edge of the plateau. When Brink exits at the powerline, go 0.1 mile south (left), and then east (right) to the entrance of Swamp Trail (P). There are boardwalks over the swampy drainage from Tradition Lake, and they can sometimes be slippery. New nature walk storyboards adorn this route. After 0.6 mile you'll find yourself back at the High Point parking lot and will have exercised every muscle and skill necessary to trail running.

SIGNIFICANT TRAIL LANDMARKS
A.   Follow West Tiger No. 3 Trail south out of the parking lot.
B.   Turn right onto Bus Trail.
C.   Turn left and up onto Nook Trail.
D.   Go right onto Connector Trail over to Section Line Trail. Go left.

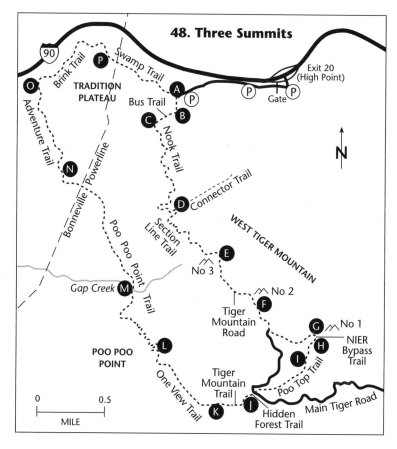

E.   West Tiger Mountain 3 summit. Trail continues down switchbacks on the south side.

F.   West Tiger Mountain 2 summit. Follow Main Tiger Mountain Road toward West Tiger No. 1.

G.   West Tiger Mountain 1 summit. Pick up the NIER Bypass Trail next to the hikers' hut.

H.   Branch onto West Tiger No. 1 Trail, headed uphill.

I.   Cross road in front of gate to enter Poo Top Trail, leading to Hidden Forest Trail.

J.   Go right on TMT at 4.9 miles.

K.   Go left on One View Trail.

L.   At 5.3 miles, Poo Poo Point Trail appears to be continuation of One View Trail.

M.   Cross a wood bridge over Gap Creek.

N.   Go right onto Adventure Trail.

O.   Go straight through under powerlines to Brink Trail.

P.   Turn left, then right through a grassy, wide path to Swamp Trail.

49 SEATTLE'S FAVORITE LOOP

Distance	16 miles
Course geometry	Loop
Running time	4 hours
Elevation gain	3700 feet
Highest altitude	2948 feet
Difficulty	Strenuous
Water	40 ounces
Restrooms	Outhouse at trailhead
Permits	None required
Area management	Department of Natural Resources (DNR)
Maps	Tiger Mountain Trails, Issaquah Alps Trail Club Guide to Trails of Tiger Mountain, Green Trails #204S, Tiger Mountain Map, DNR Washington State
Season	Year-round, snow on top sometimes in winter

Each New Year, Northwest ultrarunners join together for two loops on this route to take care of excess holiday eating. This tradition allows guilt-free meals all through the holidays. The route offers all types of running terrain and a great anytime workout. I've run this trail in all

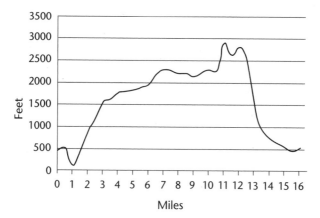

seasons and all weather, and to me it looks a little different each time. Although I may get tired, I never tire of this route.

GETTING THERE

From Interstate 90 east of Issaquah, take Exit 20 (High Point). Turn right on the frontage road and go 0.4 mile to the gate. If the gate is open and you know you will be finished running before dusk, you may continue by car 0.5 mile to the upper parking lot, otherwise park outside the gate, which closes at dusk.

THE RUN

Although the official version of this loop starts at the gate of the lower parking area, the route described here starts out the same as the Tradition Lake Plateau route (Run 46). From the lower parking lot, run up the hill and go right at the top of the road along the powerline to enter Swamp Trail (A) on the right. Continue on Swamp Trail until you see a trail on the left. Go right across the grass under the powerlines, then take a left onto Brink Trail (B). From Brink Trail, turn right again and follow the wide path under the powerline as it heads toward Issaquah. Stay on the rim, curving to the left till you pass the clear view of Issaquah, then turn right through a wooden gate onto a trail going down the cliff (C). This is a new trail, and I don't think it has a name. Follow this trail down the embankment and across the road leading to the high school. Keep going straight until you reach the Issaquah High School gym (D). Across from the gym, turn left into the woods, then quickly right, and head up the hill on the High School Trail. When you reach the top of this trail you'll see a sign marked HIGH SCHOOL. Three

Ron Nicholl takes a water break at the Paw Print rest area.

trails lead away from this point. Cross under the powerlines and take the trail on the right, Poo Poo Point Trail (E). Continue up on this trail until you reach the West Tiger Railroad Grade (F). Cross it and continue up onto One View Trail. This ends about 4 miles of almost continuous climb.

At a fork in the trail, turn right onto the Tiger Mountain Trail (TMT) (G). Continue for 2.5 miles, then turn left onto the 15-mile Railroad Grade Trail (H). This is a fairly straight trail leading to the Paw Print restroom. From Paw Print continue on the railroad grade, now labeled as the Preston Trail, for another 0.5 mile until you see an unmarked trail going off to the left. This is Bootleg Trail (I). Bootleg Trail started out as an unofficial shortcut connector trail and is unmarked at this end. This trail formerly ended on the summit of West Tiger No. 1, but with the new communications towers, it's thought to be unsafe to run through the electrical fields. A new and quite nice trail, the Non-Iodizing Electromagnetic Radiation (NIER) Bypass Trail (J) has been provided for public use. Bypass West Tiger No. 1 on this trail and come out just below the summit at a hikers' hut (K) on Main Tiger Mountain Road.

Turn right and run down the long grade, go around the gate, and start up the next grade to West Tiger No. 2. At the top of West Tiger No. 2, after you've enjoyed the superb views of Mount Rainier to the left and Squak Mountain in front of you, look for a trail to the north in the low vegetation. Follow the saddle down, then up to West Tiger No. 3. This is the most popular and easily accessible peak of Tiger Mountain, and there will almost always be hikers from this point on. Don't trample them! From this summit there are expansive views to the south, west, and north, including Lake Sammamish, Lake Washington, Bellevue, Seattle, and, on especially clear days, Puget Sound and the Olympic Mountains. The West Tiger No. 3 Trail back to the High Point parking area is to the east side of West Tiger No. 3 (L). The view to the east is an up-close look at Mount Si and the Cascade Range. Follow this trail 2.25 miles down to the powerline and upper parking lot. There is a sign that points to Tradition Lake, but you are still on the West Tiger No. 3 Trail. This grade makes for a fast and powerful finish.

SIGNIFICANT TRAIL LANDMARKS

A. Run up road from lower parking lot and go right on Swamp Trail.
B. Go right under the powerlines, then left onto Brink Trail.
C. Wooden gate leads to a trail going steeply downhill.
D. Issaquah High School gym. Go left into the woods, then quickly right up the High School Trail.

E. Go under powerlines and turn right onto Poo Poo Point Trail.

F. Cross railroad grade and go up One View Trail

G. Go right at fork onto Tiger Mountain Trail at 7.1 miles.

H. Go left onto unsigned 15-Mile Railroad Grade Trail. Cross road and continue on past restroom. Trail becomes Preston Trail.

I. At 10.4 miles, go left onto unsigned Bootleg Trail.

J. Follow the NIER Bypass Trail to the right (this isn't marked clearly; if you reach the fenced summit of West Tiger No. 1, you've gone too far).

K. Hikers' hut. Turn right onto Main Tiger Mountain Road. Follow the road to West Tiger No. 2, then look north for trail to West Tiger No. 3.

L. To the right of the West Tiger No. 3 summit, take the north trail that goes briefly into the woods then along the rocky edge. This is West Tiger No. 3 Trail, which is not marked at this writing. Follow to parking lot.

50 IVERSON RAILROAD AND NORTHWEST TIMBER TRAILS

Distance	8.5 miles
Course geometry	Out and back plus loop
Running time	2.5 hours
Elevation gain	1050 feet
Highest altitude	1710 feet
Difficulty	Easy
Water	40 ounces
Restrooms	Outhouse at trailhead
Permits	None required
Area management	Department of Natural Resources (DNR)
Maps	Issaquah Alps Trail, DNR Tiger Mountain
Season	Year-round

The south end of Tiger Mountain offers a slightly different landscape than the north. From the Highway 18 summit parking area, there is a road leading to bicycle trails and, in general, more gradually sloping terrain. You don't have to go far to find steep inclines; however, the trails mentioned here travel an east–west route along the contour with only gently rolling hills. There are abundant wildflowers in the lightly forested areas and an interpretive area that is a nice place to introduce children to some of these woods' inhabitants and activities.

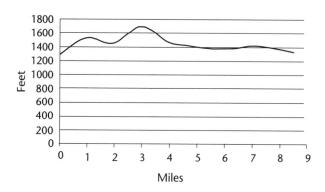

GETTING THERE
The parking lot is at the Tiger Mountain summit on State Route 18. State Route 18 can be accessed from Interstate 90 near Preston, Exit

25, or from Interstate 5 just north of Auburn, or from Maple Valley Highway. From all directions there are signs pointing to Tiger Mountain summit.

THE RUN

From the parking lot, follow the West Side Road to the left and stay on it for more than 2 miles until you reach the Iverson Railroad Trail on the right (A). This trail allows bikes from April 15 through October 15; there is little underbrush here, however, so it is fairly simple to step off the trail to allow a bike to pass. There are a couple of creeks to cross, but bridges exist where needed. This trail of gently rolling hills through dark old woods joins what is marked as the Connector Trail (B) for about 0.3 mile before the route crosses Main Tiger Mountain Road.

On the east side of the road is an entrance to the Northwest Timber Trail (C), named after the company that logged most of Tiger Mountain. This segment of trail is 2.3 miles, according to the sign at the north terminus. It goes through old-growth and 1980s-era clear-cuts. This, too, is a pleasantly rolling trail with little underbrush and a wide, flat path. At the end of this trail you come to the East Side Road (D). Turn around and head back to the junction with Main Tiger Mountain Road. Cross the road and take the Connector Trail 0.3 mile to a junction with the Iverson Railroad Trail at the trailhead. This is an 8.5-mile run.

Running along the Northwest Timber Trail

To add another 4 miles, retrace your course on Iverson, then circle back on West Side Road to the parking lot. One short detour is an interpretive loop (E) that starts and ends behind the bathrooms above the trailhead. Storyboards here relate a little about the timber industry and the flora and fauna of Tiger Mountain.

SIGNIFICANT TRAIL LANDMARKS

A. From parking lot, follow West Side Road for 2.1 miles to enter Iverson Railroad Trail on the right.
B. Iverson Railroad Trail joins Connector Trail at 4.1 miles.
C. Cross Main Tiger Mountain Road and enter Northwest Timber Trail.
D. Northwest Timber Trail ends on East Side Road. Turn around and return to Main Tiger Mountain Road. Follow Connector Trail to trailhead.
E. Interpretive loop and bathrooms.

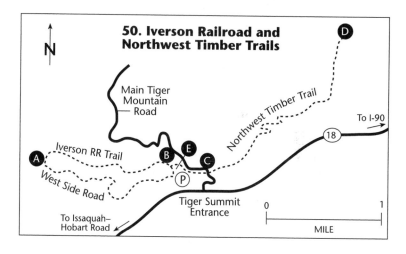

APPENDIXES

LIST OF TRAILS

Distances are in miles, elevations are in feet, and running times are in hours. Run types are out and back (OB), loop (L), and point to point (PTP).

TRAILS	DISTANCE (MILES)	TYPE	TIME (HOURS)	ELEV. GAIN (FEET)	HI ELEV. (FEET)	DIFFICULTY	SEASONS
Olympic Peninsula							
1. Quinault Loop	4	L	1.25	450	480	Easy	Year-round
2. Hurricane Hill to Elwha Ranger Station	7.5	PTP	2	730/5300	5757	Moderate	July–Oct.
3. Dosewallips to Gray Wolf Pass	25.2	OB	9	5940	6240	Strenuous	July–Oct.
Bellingham							
4. Chuckanut Mountain	18.5	L	4.5	4000	1940	Strenuous	Year-round
5. Blanchard Hill	10	OB	2.75	1830	2110	Moderate	Year-round

TRAILS	DISTANCE (MILES)	TYPE	TIME (HOURS)	ELEV. GAIN (FEET)	HI ELEV. (FEET)	DIFFICULTY	SEASONS
6. Oyster Dome	8	L	3	3000	2120	Strenuous	Year-round
7. Squires Lake	5	L	1.5	700	900	Easy	Year-round
North Cascades							
8. Baker Lake	26	OB	7	2540	990	Moderate	Year-round
9. Sauk Mountain	7.2	OB	2.5	2400	5324	Moderate	July–Oct.
10. Blue Lake	4.6	OB	1.5	800	6100	Easy	July–Oct.
11. Rainy Pass to Cutthroat Lake	18	OB	5.5	3700	6800	Strenuous	July–Oct.
12. Sun Mountain	10	L	2.5	900	2850	Easy	May–Oct.
13. Suiattle River	34	L	9	4900	6000	Strenuous	July–Oct.
14. Mount Pilchuck	6	OB	2.5	2300	5324	Moderate	July–Oct.
15. Wallace Falls	6	OB/L	2	1600	1500	Moderate	Year-round
16. Wallace Lake	13	OB	3	1500	1844	Moderate	Year-round
Central Cascades							
17. Mount Si	8	OB	2.5	3250	3900	Strenuous	Year-round
18. Denny Creek to Kaleetan Lake	19	OB	8	6260	4500	Strenuous	July–Oct.
19. McClellan Butte	8.8	OB	4	3700	5162	Strenuous	July–Oct.

20. Pratt Lake	12	OB	4	3200	4140	Moderate	July–Oct.
21. Kachess Ridge to Thorp Mountain	18	OB	6.5	6120	5854	Strenuous	June–Oct.
22. Kachess Lake to Snoqualmie Pass	27	PTP	9	6300	5730	Strenuous	July–Oct.
23. South Cle Elum Ridge	29	L	8	5600	5820	Strenuous	June–Oct.
South Cascades							
24. Norse Peak Wilderness	17	L	6.5	3420	5920	Strenuous	July–Oct.
25. Mowich Lake	17	L	6	4500	6300	Strenuous	July–Oct.
26. Wonderland Trail	17.5	OB	6	5270	6760	Strenuous	July–Oct.
Olympia							
27. Capitol Peak	9.4	OB	2.5	1550	2659	Moderate	Year-round
28. Rock Candy Mountain	18.5	L	5.5	3700	2360	Moderate	Year-round
29. Larch Mountain	7	OB	2	1200	2659	Easy	Year-round
Eastern Washington							
30. Manastash Ridge	10	OB	2.5	2140/3100	3922	Moderate	Year-round
31. Canyon Rim	16	OB	4	4200	3208	Strenuous	Year-round
32. Mount Spokane	10	OB	2.5	2230	5282	Moderate	June–Oct.
33. Dishman Hills	5	L	1.5	600	2350	Easy	March–Oct.
34. Rocks of Sharon	8	L	2	1840	3600	Moderate	March–Oct.
35. Liberty Lake Park	7	L	2.25	1340	3140	Moderate	March–Oct.

TRAILS	DISTANCE (MILES)	TYPE	TIME (HOURS)	ELEV. GAIN (FEET)	HI ELEV. (FEET)	DIFFICULTY	SEASONS
Urban Trails							
36. St. Edwards State Park	8	L	1.5	1200	390	Moderate	Year-round
37. Tolt Pipeline	16	OB	4–6	3250	1000	Moderate	Year-round
38. Redmond Watershed and Puget Powerline Trails	15	OB/L	4	1060	560	Moderate	Year-round
39. Discovery Park	2.8–8	L	0.5–2	500	300	Easy	Year-round
40. Bridle Trails State Park	4.8	L	1	260	460	Easy	Year-round
41. Lake to Lake Trail	19	OB	4.5	1500	340	Easy	Year-round
42. Point Defiance Park	9.3	L	2	200	200	Easy	Year-round
43. Snoqualmie Valley	18.8	PTP	3	1400	490	Easy	Year-round
Issaquah Alps							
44. Cougar Mountain Ring	14	L	3.75	2200	1595	Moderate	Year-round
45. Squak Mountain	8	L	2	1680	2020	Moderate	Year-round
46. Tradition Lake Plateau	6	L	1.5	600	520	Easy	Year-round
47. Twelve Summits	34	OB	11	10,500	3004	Strenuous	Year-round
48. Three Summits	10	L	2.5	3500	2948	Strenuous	Year-round
49. Seattle's Favorite Loop	16	L	4	3700	2948	Strenuous	Year-round
50. Iverson Railroad and Northwest Timber Trails	8.5	OB	2.5	1050	1710	Easy	Year-round

LIST OF REGIONAL TRAIL RUNNING EVENTS

January
Fat Ass 50K
Tiger Mountain, WA
ronn@wolfenet.com, cherig@wolfenet.com

Bridle Trails Twilight 50K
Bellevue, WA
425-828-0250
cdralph@attglobal.net
www.pws.prserv.net/CascadeRunningClub/bt50k.htm

February
Mazama Snow Shoe Shuffle
Twisp, WA
509-996-3287
www.mvsta.com

March
Chuckanut Mountain 50K
Bellingham, WA
360-671-5978
www.basecampwa.com/chuckanut50

April
Mount Si Relay & Ultra Run
Snoqualmie, WA
877-242-1634
www.ontherun.com/mtsirelay

McDonald Forest 50K Ultramarathon
Corvallis, OR
541-737-2373
www.orst.edu/groups/triclub/ultra/ultra.html

Peace Park Trail Run 5 Mile
Janeville, BC
608-756-1832

May
Sunflower Relay
Twisp, WA
www.mvsta.com

Five Peaks Trail Running Series
Vancouver, BC
604-572-4625
www.fivepeaks.com

June
Ultra-Man Trail Run/Walk Fitness Challenge
Lakewood, WA
253-376-0092
humansports2001@hotmail.com
www.trifind.com/humansports

Winterhawk 50K
Portland, OR
redrunz@juno.com

Run the Sun
Twisp, WA
509-996-3287
www.mvsta.com

July
Chuckanut Foot Race
Bellingham, WA
360-734-3953

Daybreak Climb a Mountain Run
Spokane, WA
509-927-1688
www.daybreakrun.org

White River 50 Mile Trail Run
Greenwater, WA
206-325-4800
footzonerun@yahoo.com
www.whiteriver50.org

Siskiyou Out Back (SOB) Trail Run
sob@danabandy.com

Knee Knackering North Shore Trail Run
West Vancouver, BC
604-222-3199
www.kneeknacker.com

August
Cutthroat Classic
Mazama, WA
509-996-3287
www.mvsta.com

Cascade Crest Classic 100 mile
Easton, WA
509-656-2600
randyg@eburg.com
www.ultrarunner.net

Super Energy X-Country Trail Championships
Lakewood, WA
253-376-0092
www.trifind.com/humansports

September
Cle Elum Ridge Trail Run 50K
Cle Elum, WA
206-525-1295
seafrank@seanet.com

Plain Endurance Run 100 mile
Plain, WA
425-828-0250
cdralph@attglobal.net
www.pws.prserv.net/CascadeRunningClub/plain.htm

McKenzie River Trail Run
McKenzie Bridge, OR
541-726-6203
phvaughn@pond.net

November
Ron Herzog Memorial 50K
Granite Falls, WA
425-828-0250
cdralph@attglobal.net
www.pws.prserv.net/CascadeRunningClub/ronh.htm

Dances With Turkeys Trail Run/Walk and Mountain Bike Duathlon
Challenge Benefit
Lakewood, WA
253-376-0092
humansports2001@hotmail.com
www.trifind.com/humansports

Adventure Run 10K Trail Run
St. Edwards State Park
Kenmore, WA
206-271-0652

December
Midnight Express 8K Trail Run
Lakewood, WA
253-376-0092
humansports2001@hotmail.com
www.trifind.com/humansports

INDEX

ABOUT THE AUTHOR

CHERI POMPEO GILLIS was born and raised in Washington state and has been an avid trail runner since 1996. She has run in more than 85 marathons and ultra marathons, with a top distance to date of 102 miles.

She has a Bachelor of Science degree in Physics and a Master of Science in Computer Science from the University of Washington. She regularly writes for running publications, such as *Northwest Runner, Ultrarunning Magazine,* and *www.ontherun.com.* She has also published short stories and essays in various literary journals and newspapers. She lives with her family on a quiet lake in Woodinville, Washington.

About trail running, Gillis explains that "the pervading aromas of rich soil, pine and fir needles are balm to my spirit. I started running to get in shape, but quickly fell in love with the sport and kept adding miles. There didn't seem to be a limit to the distances I could run."

THE MOUNTAINEERS, founded in 1906, is a nonprofit outdoor activity and conservation club, whose mission is "to explore, study, preserve, and enjoy the natural beauty of the outdoors. . . ." Based in Seattle, Washington, the club is now the third-largest such organization in the United States, with 15,000 members and five branches throughout Washington State.

The Mountaineers sponsors both classes and year-round outdoor activities in the Pacific Northwest, which include hiking, mountain climbing, ski-touring, snowshoeing, bicycling, camping, kayaking and canoeing, nature study, sailing, and adventure travel. The club's conservation division supports environmental causes through educational activities, sponsoring legislation, and presenting informational programs. All club activities are led by skilled, experienced volunteers, who are dedicated to promoting safe and responsible enjoyment and preservation of the outdoors.

If you would like to participate in these organized outdoor activities or the club's programs, consider a membership in The Mountaineers. For information and an application, write or call The Mountaineers, Club Headquarters, 300 Third Avenue West, Seattle, WA 98119; 206-284-6310.

The Mountaineers Books, an active, nonprofit publishing program of the club, produces guidebooks, instructional texts, historical works, natural history guides, and works on environmental conservation. All books produced by The Mountaineers Books fulfill the club's mission.

Send or call for our catalog of more than 500 outdoor titles:

The Mountaineers Books
1001 SW Klickitat Way, Suite 201
Seattle, WA 98134
800-553-4453
mbooks@mountaineersbooks.org
www.mountaineersbooks.org

The Mountaineers Books is proud to be a corporate sponsor of Leave No Trace, whose mission is to promote and inspire responsible outdoor recreation through education, research, and partnerships. The Leave No Trace program is focused specifically on human-powered (nonmotorized) recreation.

Leave No Trace strives to educate visitors about the nature of their recreational impacts, as well as offer techniques to prevent and minimize such impacts. Leave No Trace is best understood as an educational and ethical program, not as a set of rules and regulations.

For more information, visit *www.LNT.org*, or call 800-332-4100.

TRAIL RUNNER, The Magazine of Running Adventure, is the first nationally distributed, full-color magazine devoted to off-road running. It covers all aspects of trail running, from leisurely fitness runs to grueling, high-altitude ultra-marathons, as well as snowshoeing, adventure racing, and orienteering. Our mission is to inform, entertain, and invigorate trail runners of all abilities with interesting news coverage, useful training and nutritional advice, critical product reviews, and inspirational features. *Trail Runner* is published in Boulder, Colorado, by North South Publications, which also produces the award-winning climbing magazine *Rock & Ice*.

To subscribe, call toll-free 877-762-5423 or visit us online at *www.trailrunnermag.com*.